Sympathy for the Traitor

Also by Mark Polizzotti

Lautréamont Nomad
Revolution of the Mind: The Life of André Breton
The New Life: Poems
Los Olvidados
Bob Dylan: Highway 61 Revisited
Disordering My Library

As editor

André Breton: Selections
Révolutions surréalistes
They Knew What They Wanted: Poems and Collages by John Ashbery

Sympathy for the Traitor

A Translation Manifesto

Mark Polizzotti

The MIT Press
Cambridge, Massachusetts
London, England

Portions of this book have previously appeared, in substantially different form, in the essays "Traduced with Abandon: Translation and Its Malcontents" (*Parnassus* 32, spring 2011), "Sense and Serendipity: The Masochistic Art of Translating Surrealism" (*New Ohio Review* 14, fall 2013), and "The Translator's Responsibility" (*Translation Review* 96, Oct. 2016). Grateful acknowledgment is made to the editors of these periodicals.

This book was set in ITC Stone Serif Std by Toppan Best-set Premedia Limited. Printed and bound in the United States of America.

Library of Congress Cataloging-in-Publication Data is available.

ISBN: 978-0-262-03799-0

10 9 8 7 6 5 4 3 2 1

This is for Jacky

Contents

Acknowledgments

This book benefited from the exacting eyes of several early readers whose insights made it much better than it would have been, most notably Ben Downing, Jacky Colliss Harvey, William Rodarmor, Damion Searls, and Shelby Vincent. To them I express my profound gratitude.

My thanks to the editors of the periodicals that published early portions of what become these chapters: Herb Leibowitz of *Parnassus*, Jill Rosser of the *New Ohio Review*, and Rainer Schulte of *Translation Review*. I also thank Charles Hatfield, Associate Director of the Center for Translation Studies at the University of Texas, Dallas; Marilyn Kallet, Director of the Creative Writing Program at the University of Tennessee; and the poet and translator Clayton Eshleman, in his capacity as visiting professor at UCLA, for giving me a chance to road-test some of my ideas in their graduate seminars.

At MIT Press, I'm grateful to my editor and fellow translator Marc Lowenthal, who commissioned this book and has provided advice through its various stages, and to production editor Marcy Ross and copy editor David Hill for their help in bringing the text to its final form.

Various friends and colleagues have inspired me and helped shaped my thinking over the years with their writings, thoughts, guidance, and conversation, in particular Esther Allen, Harold Augenbraum, David Bellos, Rika Lesser, Ron Padgett, Trevor Winkfield, and Bill Zavatsky.

Thank you to my parents, Mario and Grace Polizzotti, for many years of support and encouragement; to my son, Alex Polizzotti, for enthusiastic curiosity about this project since the beginning; and to my partner, Jacky Colliss Harvey, for listening to its many iterations with consummate grace and much-needed reassurance.

Finally, I will always be indebted to Jean-Louis Bouttes and Maurice Roche, who (however inadvertently) first set me on the path of translation, one from which I've never looked back.

Introduction: Ground Rules

For some, translation is the poor cousin of literature, fool's gold or last resort, a necessary evil if not an outright travesty. For others, it is the royal road to cross-cultural understanding and literary enrichment. Translation skirts the boundaries between art and craft, originality and replication, altruism and commerce, even between genius and hack work. Vladimir Nabokov (himself a noted translator) tarred the pursuit as "A parrot's screech, a monkey's chatter, / And profanation of the dead," while writers such as Ezra Pound, Samuel Beckett, Robert Lowell, Elizabeth Bishop, Kenneth Rexroth, Ted Hughes, John Ashbery, Lydia Davis, and Harry Mathews—not to mention Charles Baudelaire, Jorge Luis Borges, Osip Mandelstam, Boris Pasternak, Paul Celan, Cesare Pavese, Yves Bonnefoy, Haruki Murakami, and Peter Handke—have produced translations that are literary marvels in their own right. At a time when the globe is just a mouse click away; when authors such as Roberto Bolaño, Karl Ove Knausgaard, Patrick Modiano, Elena Ferrante, Stieg Larsson, Clarice Lispector, Umberto Eco, and Marguerite Duras, to name only a few, have staked important claims in the American literary landscape; and when translation is recognized as being ever more relevant, it is remarkable how many misconceptions still cling to it.

This book began in response both to those misconceptions and to the increasingly abstract discourse that surrounds translation studies. My goal is to reframe the debate along more fruitful lines; to address the checkered reputation translation has acquired over centuries of literary, linguistic, and philological scholarship; to share some of the problems and solutions I've discovered in the course of translating more than fifty books in nearly as many years; and to sensitize readers, both those with an informed interest and those with little notion at all, not only to the many components and challenges that go into translation but also to its central importance. The fact is, much of how we use language, how we think and structure our world, the news reports we read, the classics we study, are due to some form of translation. Without translation, we would know far less than we do, would not have encountered many of the texts we take for granted and that form the basis of our "national" culture, and would have an even more parochial and isolated view of our place in the vast flow of humanity. More than anything, I hope to sketch a portrait of the art and craft of translation that will help readers see it less as a problem to be solved, more as (when done well) an achievement to be celebrated—or, as Goethe memorably put it in a letter to Thomas Carlyle, "one of the weightiest and worthiest affairs in the general concerns of the world."[1]

Rather than trying to provide definitive answers—which I don't believe exist—I hope to bring the main questions into clearer focus: What is the ultimate goal of a translation? What does it mean to label a rendering "faithful" or "unfaithful," and how useful are those criteria? What are the translator's ethical responsibilities toward the reader and toward the source text? Is something inevitably "lost" in translation, and can something also be gained? Can and should a translation ever improve upon the original? What makes some versions sing and others screech? And, ultimately, does translation matter, and if so, why does it matter?

There are many adequate histories of translation, and this brief study does not claim to be one of them, though I do devote one chapter to a very selective historical overview. Similarly, I am not concerned with adaptations of works into other media, such as *The Great Gatsby* resurfacing as a pop song or *À la recherche du temps perdu* as a graphic novel. While there is an argument to be made for considering each of these a form of translation— as does Roman Jakobson, for instance—it would also have led us away from my primary focus. Translation even in the strictly linguistic sense is complex enough.

As an additional disclaimer, I should note that those looking for a flashy new theory need not bother reading any further: there are plenty of them out there, from the prescriptive to the prohibitive (not to mention the plainly abstruse), and I don't intend to add to the noise. Consider this rather an "antitheory," or perhaps just a common-sense approach. I'm aware that common sense isn't nearly as exciting as taking an extreme position. But having perused a number of extreme positions, I've found them not of much use when it comes to looking at what translation is—or, as the translator David Bellos puts it, what it *does*—and many of them aren't even very exciting brain teasers.

My aim, instead, is to encourage you to think differently about translation, and to provide pointers on how to read not only translations per se but also the act of translation itself. Consider this book a manual and a manifesto—an unabashedly opinionated examination of what translation is and isn't, and how it does or doesn't work, from a pragmatic, philosophical, historical, ethical, aspirational, performative, economic, practical, polemical, interrogative, and, I trust, resolutely unfashionable standpoint. To avoid confusion, I'll state at the outset that I derive most of my examples and problematics from the English-speaking world, usually North America, and that the word *translation* is primarily shorthand for literary translation, though I have also taken examples from other disciplines when appropriate. And while many instances come from my experience with French, the points they are illustrating are meant to apply to other languages as well.

Two guiding principles obtain throughout the discussion that follows. The first is that translators are creative artists in their own right, on a par, and in partnership, with the author being translated. The renowned Spanish translator Gregory Rabassa has posited that the translator is "the ideal writer because all he has to do is write; plot, theme, characters, and all the other essentials have already been provided, so he can just sit down and write his ass off."[2] While the position is by no means universally accepted, it provides a useful lens through which to gauge the importance, responsibilities, and limitations of translation. The second principle is that translation is a *practice*. For all the many fascinating theoretical approaches one can take to the subject, I believe that ultimately it's the end result that counts, the fruit of an activity.

In my four decades as an active translator, I've had the opportunity to work with everything from experimental fiction (undertaken when I was too young to know better) to mainstream thrillers, philosophy to technical manuals, biographies to poetry, art history to political analysis. I've encountered a number of challenges, and also quite a few instances of sheer luck. What these various efforts have taught me is that while certain basic questions recur time and time again—having to do with voice, approach, readership, the strictures one must observe, and the liberties one can take—the answers are rarely the same from case to case. Every new book requires its own rethinking of the problems at hand, and, though certain guidelines might prove helpful, no theory or dogma can replace the translator's work of grappling with the text on its own terms, of devising an appropriate strategy. In other words, and despite the claims of many commentators from ancient times down to the present day, there is no magic, one-size-fits-all method. As in all writing, laws are made, broken, and made again; with each new project we reinvent the proverbial wheel. If there is a ground rule of translation, it might simply be that there are no ground rules.

1 Is Translation Possible (and What Is It, Anyway)?

At its most basic level, the translator's task can be defined as the self-effacing re-creation in one language of a text produced in another. The key word in that sentence is *self-effacing*, expressing the supposed ideal that the original author's voice will emerge intact, though using different words, through the transformative screen that another writer has erected for it. There are, of course, translations that have become famous as such, from Edward FitzGerald's *Rubáiyát* to Ezra Pound's *Cathay*; and widely recognized translators, such as Constance Garnett, Ralph Manheim, William Weaver, Edith Grossman, Gregory Rabassa, Ann Goldstein, Linda Coverdale, and Richard Howard, their renown sometimes greater than the author's. But more often than not, toilers in the translation fields, however talented, remain hidden to all but the eagle-eyed few, silent and invisible and ready to serve, like footmen at a soirée.[1]

As it happens, the work of translation isn't as self-effacing as you might think. Indeed, throughout history, some of the most celebrated and beautifully realized translations have been successful precisely because the personality of the translator shone through and made itself felt. Re-creating someone else's text (or even your own, if you happen to be a Beckett or Nabokov) is less a matter of following the original line by line—replacing each word with its nearest equivalent as if they were carpet tiles—than of conveying what's between those lines, and this takes a certain amount of interpretation, not to say idiosyncrasy. Even apparently seamless transitions from one idiom, one cultural context, one set of historical and popular assumptions into another; even fluidly rendered descriptive passages and snatches of natural-sounding dialogue, are the product of many weighed choices, of phrasings discarded, reinstated, and discarded again. Making something look effortless is hard work. It takes only a mildly botched or flat-footed job to demonstrate how much decision and, yes, art go into an inspired one. Good translators, like the good authors they render, approach their efforts with a healthy dose of creativity and reflection. While a translator will always have to confront the nitty-gritty of, say, suggesting gendered nouns in a language that has none, more often than not she also has to grapple with a number of methodological, philosophical, and even ethical choices, including the choice of just how "seamless" that transition should appear.

Let's unpack the other assumption in that initial sentence: that a translation aims to reproduce in one language what a given author said in another. The first problem lies in defining those terms. Is "what the author said" the literal meaning? The connotations? The effect on the reader? The cultural, linguistic, or historical associations? The sonority of the language? All of the above? Does this transmission take place on the level of words? Of sentences? Of paragraphs? And how does one convey such things, especially when leaping between what might be two very distant branches of the linguistic tree? As these questions suggest, translation in the best sense, far from being a rote exercise, is a constantly shifting evaluation of priorities, in which the translator combs through the available resources and draws, like a Method actor, upon his own experience in order to voice the original author's utterances credibly.

Needless to say, not all translations require deep research or dazzling feats of linguistic legerdemain. Some works slip fairly handily into another tongue. But for most texts, even the ostensibly "simple" ones, a successful translation is the product of much trial, error, revision, and even invention, for sometimes the "target" or "receiving" language simply offers no direct equivalent, either in vocabulary or in mindset, and the solution must be reached circuitously. (Moreover, a frequent paradox is that the most straightforward texts can pose the biggest challenges. Says Alice Kaplan, "Like a simple melody on the piano, a simple prose style in the original exposes the translator. It can be much harder to play.")[2]

Even more fundamental, in that it influences the entire nature of the translation in question, is the matter of whether one should ultimately side with the original or "source" text or with the sometimes conflicting needs of its target-language re-creation. The ticklish issue of where to pledge one's fealty tends to split translators into two camps: on the one side, those who feel that the author's meaning and form, syntax and idiomatic peculiarities, must be scrupulously respected, even if it means doing violence to the receiving language's conventions; and on the other, those who argue that the translation must produce an effect on its audience similar to that produced by the original, which sometimes requires deviating from the strict confines of that original in order to preserve its spirit or "flavor."

The literal-versus-liberal controversy stretches back virtually as far as translation itself. At the turn of the first millennium, the lyric poet Horace was already enjoining translators "not

[to] seek to render word for word" (a sentiment that Sir John Denham echoed in 1648, when he praised a translation for not following "That servile path ... / Of tracing word by word, and line by line"). At around the same time as Horace, the orator Cicero offered this prescription for the translation of speeches: "I did not think it necessary to translate word for word, but I have kept the force and flavor of the passage." Five centuries later, taking the opposite tack, the Roman statesman and philosopher Boethius argued for a strictly literal rendering, placing "uncorrupted truth" firmly over "the grace of a beautiful style."[3]

Further muddying the waters are the agendas of those who write, promote, or publish translations. The scholar, for whom a translation is mainly a pedagogical crib, will follow Boethius by insisting on a sense-for-sense equivalent, stylistic niceties be damned (just as Boethius himself was mainly concerned with philosophical texts and their precise meanings). But others have had different priorities. The Romans, for instance, had no qualms about freely adapting Greek orations to fit the norms of good Latin, since they valued them largely as models for their own oratory and fodder for their own literary culture (even as the Greeks helped promote this spread of their literature into the Roman world).[4] In recent centuries, it was not uncommon for a translator offended by some passage to bowdlerize it in the interests of market acceptability or personal squeamishness, and nowadays publishers routinely gloss over anything deemed too foreign so as to make their books more audience-friendly. These competing agendas, and the adaptations and compromises they entail, are what fuel much of the exhausting but seemingly inexhaustible debate over whether translation is "possible" at all.

The question of whether translation is or isn't possible, and to what degree, and how much is "lost" in it, and just what that means, has been exercising translators and translation watchers practically since the dawn of human language, or at least since humans noticed they had more than one language at their disposal. Over the years, not only many scholars but even some practicing translators have gone out of their way to denigrate translation as a mug's game, judging by the self-defeating discourse they maintain when commenting on it. The *eppur si muove* response is, of course it's possible—translations are realized every day, in all sorts of contexts. Umberto Eco once noted that "every sensible and rigorous theory of language shows that a perfect translation is an impossible dream. In spite of this, people translate."[5]

That said, it would be utopian to pretend that the reader of a translation is truly experiencing the original, or that in the reading of any translation there isn't a degree of difference—*difference* rather than *loss*—between the text being translated and the translation itself. The heart of the matter lies in whether we conceive of a translation as a practical outcome or an unattainable ideal. If the latter, then the inherent and inevitable flaws of the translation enterprise would, in fact, make the entire effort seem futile. (But couldn't one say the same of any piece of writing?) The Spanish philosopher Ortega y Gasset noted that while translation is no doubt a "utopian task," it is only so because "everything Man does is utopian." Wishing to cut through this Gordian knot, the French philosopher Paul Ricoeur recommends that we reach the stage of acceptance, explicitly likening this to the work of mourning, and "give up the ideal of the perfect translation" once and for all.[6]

When I translate Patrick Modiano, with his deceptively plain-spoken style, I try to absorb his sensibility, internalize his structure, plot, characterization, syntax, rhythm—all the elements that Modiano put into creating his text—so as to deliver to his English-language readers the same reading experience as is had by their French-language counterparts. Needless to say, that's a pipe dream.

For one thing, languages, as we know, are not just collections of definitions and grammatical rules but instead are conditioned by a host of other factors—history, culture, usage, literary tradition, politics, chance occurrence, even something as inane as the latest celebrity scandal—and all of these factors cause words and phrases to have their own resonance, their own subtext, which moreover evolves over time. The reciprocity of culture and language, thought patterns and language, perception and language, national character and language, has been a staple of linguistic theory for centuries, from Herder to Humboldt, Coleridge to Sapir, Wittgenstein to Whorf. To remind ourselves that a nation's literature is shaped, in its form and in its essence, by the ambient language is merely to restate the obvious. "Whether consciously or unconsciously," writes George Steiner, "every act of human communication is based on a complex, divided fabric which may, fairly, be compared to the image of a plant deeply and invisibly rooted or of an iceberg largely under water."[7]

For another, and perhaps more to the point, the translated text is a collaboration. It's not the same as the original but is by necessity a reinterpretation, a second writer's reading and re-creation of the first writer's sentences, in other words an unavoidably subjective process—which is why, when I talk about Modiano's English readers, I really mean *ours*, his and mine. (Moreover, in many cases, there is a third writer in the mix as well, the line editor, who revises the translator's work and further alters its representation in the target language.) Much as I hate to admit it, my version of Modiano is no more purely "him" than Barbara

Wright's, or Joanna Kilmartin's, or Damion Searls's, or any of the other translators who have tried their hand at his books. With varying degrees of success, each of us has brought Modiano's voice into English; and in so doing, each of us has unavoidably infused that voice with tonalities of our own.

Arguably, it is this constantly shifting balance between objective fact (the text to be translated) and subjective interpretation (a given translator's version of it) that accounts for the persistence and vehemence of the conviction that translation is inherently impossible. It rests on a conception of human language that considers speech merely a conveyer of information, or, as David Bellos puts it, a "desire to believe (despite all evidence to the contrary) that words are at bottom the names of things."[8] As Bellos notes, this conception goes all the way back to the Book of Genesis, in which Adam sets about naming "every living creature"—which begs the question of how Adam would have named a particular shade of blue (or indigo, or azure) hovering over the Paris skyline at dusk, or the feeling of melancholy (wistfulness, gloom) that might visit you at that hour. Nor does it account for the fact that even supposedly straightforward nouns, such as *dog*, have different resonances in different cultures, even if they designate the same species. And, finally, it leaves aside the fact that, as a translator, my choice of rendering the French word *chien* as *dog*, *hound*, *cur*, *pooch*, *canine*, or *mutt* will alter the feel of my English sentence, and that one of my tasks is to decide which of those options is the most appropriate to the given context. Language is not all about designation. Its real meanings often hover in the spaces between utterances, in the movement generated by particular arrangements of words, associations, and hidden references. This is what literature does, in the best of cases. And it's what translation can do as well.

But perhaps more than anything, the conviction of translation's impossibility rests on a monolithic conception of how we read a work of literature, which logically leads one to conclude that a work's single, inalterable reading cannot be reproduced accurately in another language and culture. The reality, however, is that reading, even within a single culture, is by nature a subjective and active process. Every reader, like every translator, "loses" something in experiencing an author's work—through misunderstanding, or inattention, or personal bias, or any number of other factors—and at the same time brings something to it that no one else could bring. Even without the added white noise that the source work carries in its wake—such as previous critical acclaim, commercial success, or scandalous controversy—we can never know how target readers will react to a translation because we don't know how source readers have reacted or will react to the original from one reading to the next. If we think of the source text not as a defined, monolithic whole that can never be replicated adequately, but rather as a zone of energy, always in flux, endlessly prone to different assimilations and interpretations, then we begin to understand better the work of translation, which, like any communicative act, shows itself to be not only possible but dynamic.

***

Even accepting that translation is technically possible, there is still the matter of its place in the literary hierarchy. Darkening any gloss on translation is the shadow of the original text, towering up "like a lifeless block of resistance."[9] The dividing line between original and translation has been one of the assumed constants of translation theory and commentary, as jealously guarded as the frontier between two hostile nations, and rarely challenged. This supposedly inviolable border, however, is not an eternal verity: for centuries, from the Romans, who appropriated Greek literature, down to Chaucer and Shakespeare, who freely drew upon and adapted foreign writings as their own, it was common for so-called original works to incorporate large portions of texts from other languages, or even to swallow them entire.* Around the early seventeenth century, however, attitudes began to change. Not only did the distinction between original and translation harden, but the sacred authority of the original was established.

One reason for this attitude is technological: the rise of the printing press and the printed book brought forward the identity of the book's creator, which prioritized the notion of authorship and along with it the author's claim of copyright. Another is philosophical, stemming from both Biblical tradition and the Platonic notion of poetry as being divinely inspired and therefore levels above any attempt to replicate it. Still another has to do with the uses of translation as a pedagogical tool. Susan Bassnett suggests that classical education in particular fostered the primacy of the original by defining a "faithful" translation as an exact rendering of the original's syntax, grammar, and vocabulary, mainly as a way of demonstrating the student's knowledge of Greek and Latin. And further widening the gap

---

* The notion of "swallowing" was given more explicit currency in the twentieth century by the Brazilian "cannibalistic approach," which overtly claimed to "devour" foreign texts and revitalize them by absorbing them into a specifically Brazilian experience. "Any past which is an 'other' for us ... deserves to be eaten," the Brazilian poet Haroldo de Campos proclaimed in 1963, noting that the cannibal "devoured only the enemies he considered strong, to take from them the marrow and protein to fortify and renew his own natural energies" (Haroldo de Campos, quoted in Bassnett, *Translation*, 53–54).

are the economics of translation, which, particularly in English-speaking countries, have led to a history of notoriously low-paid pieceworkers, often mere hacks, who (judging on the evidence) considered their contract fulfilled and pittance earned if they more or less conveyed the author's basic plot, without worrying too much about the fine points. "It seems to me, that the true reason, why we have so few versions which are tolerable," John Dryden lamented in the seventeenth century, is that "there are so few, who have all the Talents, which are requisite for Translation, and that there is so little Praise, and so small Encouragement, for so considerable a part of Learning."[10]

Finally, and regardless of the translator's talent, perhaps the most resistant aspect of the divide between translation and original derives from the fact that translation, by introducing one or more additional actors into the process, poses an uncomfortable challenge to our most deep-seated and cherished notions of how art is created. If we consider a work of art to be the unique expression of the artist's inner resources, then any adaptation of it, any reworking by an outside agency (translator, film director, dramaturg) can only be seen as a pale imitation, more or less indicative of the "real thing" but by definition inferior to it.

Rather than see this as a drawback, I recommend we consider it a liberation, an acknowledgment that the translator, freed from the invidious task of trying to establish exact equivalences, can now concentrate on the much more rewarding, and perfectly possible, task of doing justice to the source text by bringing her own talents to its cause. Moreover, as has been repeatedly shown since the dawn of Modernism, art is not necessarily a singular, solitary process; rather, to borrow Lautréamont's phrase, it can just as well "be made by all, not by one" and still remain perfectly valid as art. Examples abound, in works ranging from

Lautréamont's own *Poésies* (from which this quote comes) to Max Ernst's collages to hip-hop remixes to Pound's *Cantos* to Bob Dylan's songs, in which the generated and the acquired are tightly intertwined. Even originals that are supposedly sui generis actually incorporate utterances and antecedents from a host of ages and cultures. In other words, like a translation, the source text is itself based on previous works.

Again, this is not to say that there's no significant difference between a translation and its source. What we *can* question is the longstanding value system, by recognizing what the translator's literary skills bring to the mix. To present a work as aptly as possible, to re-create it in all its beauty and ugliness, takes sensitivity, empathy, flexibility, attentiveness, and tact. And, perhaps most of all, it takes respect for one's own work, the belief that one's translation is worth judging on its own merits (or flaws), and that, if done properly, it can stand shoulder to shoulder with the source text.

No doubt such an assertion will provoke indignant guffaws from those who value above all the writer's individuality, the unique ideas expressed, the new emotions wrenched from the reader, the unprecedented social and political aperçus. How, you might ask, can I possibly equate inventing characters out of thin air, or weaving together complex strands of plot, or composing verses sweeter than honey, with mere thesaurus grubbing? This is a good question, and I don't mean to overstate my case. It's true that having to create something out of nothing is not among the translator's duties. One could take this as proof of the author's superiority over the translator. But one could just as easily not.

With due acknowledgment of the creative impetus, the simple, tautological fact is that writing, *all* writing, is at bottom a function of language. Making the reader laugh or cry, and the *way* of making this happen, ultimately depends not only on the writer's imagination but also, and perhaps even more, on the ability—be it deliberate or instinctive—to manipulate words and sounds. "Writing is not the reality it describes but the words used to name that reality,"[11] Suzanne Jill Levine aptly notes. In that regard, translators are up against the same challenges, and must bring to bear the same resources, as the authors they translate. In translating as in writing, our medium is words—words exotic or plain, common or recondite, that in their virtually infinite combinations form the mental pictures we see, the cadences we hear, and that communicate to another person just what it is we intend him to experience.

***

Given the pervasiveness of negative attitudes toward translation, ranging from grudging tolerance to outright animosity, it's worth looking more closely at where all this hostility comes from.

From the reader's viewpoint, it's not hard to understand. Reading a foreign author's text through the mediation of a translator involves a certain amount of trust, especially since most readers of translations have little or no familiarity with the source language and culture. But trust is a hard commodity to build, in any interpersonal communication, and all too easy to ruin. No one likes taking another person's word, and yet in translation, that is literally what the reader is asked to do. The stale Italian pun *traduttore, traditore* ("translator = traitor"), which has been afflicting translation commentary for centuries, derives much of its longevity from the underlying suspicion across many cultures that the middleman is either incompetent or up to no good.

The hostility is easy to understand from the author's viewpoint as well. Authors devote time and effort to crafting sentences, paragraphs, rhythms, that convey exactly what they mean to convey, on every level, semantic, syntactic, and symbolic. Bringing in another wordsmith, with whom the author often has little or no personal contact, is bound to raise suspicions—which some translators, moreover, are ill-placed to calm. As Peter Cole points out, there is also an inherent ego clash between two authors, the writer-artist and the translator-artist: "Artists are notorious for their (necessary) egoism. And strong artists are distinguished, well, by their strength—which consists, in part, of their resistance to possession by the spirit of another artist."[12] Cole is speaking here of the translator's resistance to the source writer's voice, but the claim could go both ways.

Needless to say, not all writers share this resistance. Jorge Luis Borges, for one, wondered whether the translator's craft wasn't "more subtle, more civilized than the writer's." Eco spoke admiringly of the "process of negotiation" involved in bringing *The Name of the Rose* into successful English. The French critic and novelist Maurice Blanchot considered translators "writers of the rarest sort, truly without peers." And Günter Grass famously convened all of his translators for an *Übersetzertreffen*, a several-day symposium, to confront problems and discuss possible solutions across several languages. Sometimes, writer and translator work in concert, either literally as collaborators or through sustained contact that can act as a spur to raise one's game. Edmund Keeley, the co-translator of George Seferis, has recalled that the author's "sometimes heavy shadow was always behind us in our work, or so I felt. And just to remind us that his English wasn't all that bad, the poet would occasionally send a postcard from his latest diplomatic outpost ... correcting this or that mistranslation of a word or phrase."[13] In my case, most of the living authors I've translated have kept a benevolent and trusting distance, available when needed but otherwise unobtrusive. In fact, the one instance when I did feel hampered was in translating Flaubert, whose ghost I could sense hovering over my shoulder, shaking his walrus moustache at my every *mot injuste*.

Often, however, authors will take a more distant, if not frankly antipathetic, stance toward this recasting of their works. At the laissez-faire end of the scale, they might simply assume that the translator knows what she's doing and leave it at that; or else dismiss the translated edition as merely a fringe benefit, a source of extra income and readership. At the other end are those who view the entire process with irremediable distrust. Among these is Milan Kundera, who in the dourly titled *Testaments Betrayed* (*traduttore, traditore* all over again) dissects what he considers to be faults committed by French translators of Kafka—and, by extension, by all translators. Faults of style: "For a translator, the supreme authority should be the *author's personal style*. But most translators obey another authority: that of the *conventional version* of 'good French' (or good German, good English, etc.)." Faults of composition: "The need to use another word in place of the more obvious, more simple, more neutral one ... may be called the *synonymizing reflex*—a reflex of nearly all translators. ... This practice of synonymization seems innocent, but its systematic quality inevitably smudges the original idea. And besides, what the hell for? Why not say 'go' when the author says '*gehen*'?"[14]

It's true that supposed flaws such as word repetitions and unorthodox phrasings, when they serve a stylistic or thematic function, are part and parcel of what a conscientious translator will and should try to preserve. But sometimes repetitions are just mistakes, and the translator can do better—and thereby do better by the text. The venerable word-for-word approach— essentially what Kundera is advocating—also neglects the fact that while *gehen* might fit beautifully into Kafka's German sentences in every instance, in English there might be moments when *go* works better, others when Joseph K. should *leave*, and still others when he's got to *move*. According to most current estimates, modern English offers a functional vocabulary of more than 500,000 words, three times as many as German (at around 185,000) and five times as many as French (fewer than 100,000), making it the most diverse language in the world.[15] Given this, a translator into English could find perfectly valid reasons to vary that "*gehen*."

Kundera also ridicules the translator's tendency to "enrich the vocabulary" of his version as an ego trip, a way to win kudos: "The public will automatically see richness of vocabulary as a value, as a performance, a proof of the translator's mastery and competence."[16] Granted, translators, like anyone else, crave applause, and even the best-intentioned of us might sometimes overdo it. But the fact is, writing *is* a performance, and the translator's competence *is* always at issue. As is the author's competence, as put forward by that translator. This is especially true when a foreign writer is being introduced to a new culture, but not only: the Japanese novelist and translator Haruki Murakami, who retranslated *The Great Gatsby* out of frustration with existing versions, speaks of bringing his "imaginative powers as a novelist into play" in order "to convey the power of Fitzgerald's prose. To fully grasp its essence, I had to plunge into its heart."[17] In my own case, I've worked with some authors who gladly endorsed the bits of creativity I was able to bring to the translation, just as there have been many others for whom no such alteration seemed warranted. The trick lies in knowing when such an amendment constitutes an improvement, congruent with the author's intent as best one can interpret it, and when it's simply gilding the proverbial lily, or flattering one's self-esteem.

Whether or not an English or French Kafka will have the same acid tang as in German, the same slightly off-kilter quality that marks the original, depends more than anything on the translator's ability to feel the text, intuit the extent to which he can use, and if need be abuse, the stuff of his target language. But there is a caveat, especially in translating an author with an idiosyncratic writing style: Kafka can bend German as much as he likes, but if his first English translators had done so, how was the reader to know whether they had faithfully reproduced their author's idiosyncrasies or merely botched their assignment?

While it is not the translator's task (or, one would assume, desire) to subvert the source text by, say, rendering plain, Hemingwayesque diction with verbal arabesques, crafting a beautiful sentence in order to credibly represent the beauty of the original sentence does sometimes involve a bit of performance, and perhaps a bit of enrichment as well. Shakespeare is always Shakespeare, but Lear performed by a gifted actor is simply *better* Shakespeare than when performed by a dud.

Still, we can at least leave the theater feeling we have "seen" Shakespeare, while the conviction persists even among many sophisticated consumers of literature that reading an author in translation is not *really* reading him at all. It's true that we haven't read the exact words—of course—but if the translation is performed well, we will have read the essence of what the author meant us to read, and with equal reward. To recognize this will take a shift in the way many people view translation as a whole. As long as the utopian and counterproductive fantasy of exact equivalence holds sway; as long as we take for granted that the original is necessarily of greater authority than the translation; as long as we see translation as either functionally impossible or merely utilitarian in nature, then our experience of it will remain skewed, incomplete, and unsatisfying.

2   Saints, Martyrs, and Spies

The English word *translation*, which first entered the language around the mid-fourteenth century, derives from the Latin noun *translatio* (from the verb *transferre*, "to carry across"). In the Romance languages, the root of the various terms for translation traces to a different Latin verb, *traducere*, which also means "to bring across" or "to lead beyond." Both are related to the Greek root term for *metaphor*, which, similarly, means "to carry over" or "to transfer."[1] While today that transfer mainly indicates a movement between two languages—the routine metaphor for translation is as a "bridge" between cultures or nations—initially the meaning of *translation* was to transfer a holy relic from one place to another, or else to carry a saintly figure to heaven without the intermediary of death.

Given the word's ecclesiastical and spiritual underpinnings, it is hardly surprising that the first translations in the modern sense, at least in the Western canon, were versions of the Bible. In the beginning was the Word, which then had to be adapted for a popular readership. Indeed, many of the theories and debates surrounding contemporary translation, including the ur-debate of fidelity versus felicity, can be traced back to the

early biblical translations—including the version we might call
the first mass-market translation, made in the third century BC
from the Hebrew into Koiné Greek. It was known as the Septuagint because it had purportedly been translated in seventy (or
seventy-two) days by seventy (or seventy-two) Hellenistic Jewish scholars, who, though working in separate cells, produced
identical texts—a proof of divine intervention that left the
Septuagint enviably immune to criticism and competition for,
appropriately enough, the next seven hundred years. Given its
heavenly provenance, the Septuagint was considered even more
authoritative than its source—a translator's dream—and it was
the Greek, rather than the Hebrew, that served as the basis for
subsequent Latin versions.[2]

As literature, the Septuagint offered a rather stilted reading
experience, but it faced no serious challenge until the year 384,
when Eusebius Hieronymus, the future Saint Jerome, undertook
a new Latin translation based on the Hebrew and Aramaic source
texts, bypassing the Greek. Jerome, though a devout servant of
Scripture, also understood the virtues of readability, and his
remarks on the subject show a thoroughly modern appreciation
for "the grace of something well said," as well as for the difficulty
of attaining it:

> If I translate word for word, it sounds absurd; if from necessity, I
> change something in the word-order or in the language, I am seen
> to abdicate the responsibility of a translator. ... The difficulty of the
> task is attested to by the fact that the inspired volumes produced
> by the Septuagint translators have not kept their flavor in Greek. ...
> [The] Sacred Scripture seemed so rough and uncouth that educated
> people, not knowing that it had been translated from the Hebrew,
> looked at the surface instead of the real meat and were put off by the
> unprepossessing clothing of its style rather than finding the beautiful
> body underneath.[3]

Predictably, Jerome's version yielded a flavor quite unlike what the flock had previously tasted; also predictably, it soon aroused the suspicions of his fellow theologian Aurelius Augustinus (later Saint Augustine of Hippo), whose passion for ferreting out heresies and fierce devotion to maintaining the Christian status quo suggests a medieval J. Edgar Hoover. Fearing a schism in the Faith, and perhaps aiming to ensure that the Hebrew tradition should "survive but not thrive," the future polemicist of *City of God* reprimanded Jerome for his departure from orthodoxy and argued for the maintenance of a single, inalterable, unassailable document. "Honestly," he wrote, "I would rather you translate the Scriptures for us from the canonical texts which the seventy translators left us. For it will cause extreme difficulty if your translation is widely adopted: the Latin churches will then differ violently from the Greek churches."[4] Jerome approached translation with a poet's ear; Augustine, with a bureaucrat's eagle eye. Their opposing stances make them, quite literally, the patron saints of an all-too-human debate that rages to this day.

Indeed, the Bible resurfaces time and again in the history of translation as the *locus classicus* of a conflict between those for whom the language of God is an unchanging law, to be preserved and regulated by the happy few, and those who favor flexibility and open access. Jerome's version fell in the latter camp; known as the Vulgate, it boasted the particular feature of letting the Bible be read in the more accessible Latin tongue, and eventually it replaced the Septuagint as the authoritative text. But the debate did not end there.

A thousand or so years later, in 1522, Martin Luther opened the same can of worms by rendering the New Testament into a radically simplified, "sweet and good" German that was intelligible to the common man. Goethe later commented with respect to Luther that "if you want to influence the masses, a simple translation is always best." Luther's user-friendly translation was very much in the spirit of Jerome—ironic, given that Luther was an Augustinian friar—and, like Jerome's Vulgate, it aroused the ire of the Church fathers. Also like the Vulgate, it had an enormous impact—not only on the course of organized religion, by helping displace the ecclesiastical elite, but also on the development of a unified German language and national identity, by providing it with a standardized form of expression.[5]

Soon after the publication of Luther's New Testament, and directly influenced by it, the English scholar William Tyndale published his own translation of the New Testament, which similarly aimed at bringing the Scriptures to the common reader, and took the opportunity to damn the clerics as "malicious and wily hypocrites."[6] Like Jerome and Luther before him, Tyndale ran afoul of the sitting clergy, notably Sir Thomas More, who assumed the Augustinian role of scold, and then some; tracked down while in hiding abroad, Tyndale was convicted of heresy in 1536, executed by strangulation, then burned at the stake. As it happens, More was not there to witness the punishment, having been beheaded on charges of treason three months before. (An earlier attempt to render the Bible into the English vernacular, by John Wycliffe, had also resulted in his being declared a heretic and his body being burned, though not until decades after he died by natural causes.)

"Lord! Open the King of England's eyes," Tyndale is reported to have cried out in his final moments. The following century, it was indeed a king of England who rehabilitated Tyndale's enterprise, when the latter's translation was used as model for the Authorized, or King James, Version, one of the most influential texts ever written. Conceived in 1603 and first published in 1611, the King James Bible was intended to be both stylistically beautiful, in the manner of Jerome, and, as Augustine had prescribed, authoritative enough to unite the Church under a uniform text—a readable Septuagint, as it were. And, like Tyndale's New Testament, it was intended to *speak* to the common worshipper—literally, as it was geared toward public recitation. "Translation it is that openeth the window, to let in the light," the King James authors wrote in their preface. "Indeed without translation into the vulgar tongue, the unlearned are … as that person mentioned by Isaiah, to whom when a sealed book was delivered, with this motion, 'Read this, I pray thee,' he was fain to make this answer, 'I cannot, for it is sealed.' " The translation historian Teo Savory pronounced the Authorized Version "unlikely to be superseded by any other as long as the English language is spoken or read, a claim which can hardly be made for any other translation in the literature of the world."[7] And in fact, many consider the King James Bible to be one of the crowning splendors of English literature, regardless of its origins. The number of its inventions that have now entered common parlance—from *stumbling block* and *eat, drink, and be merry* to *scapegoat, the root of all evil*, and *woe is me*—is virtually unparalleled.

Still, though the Authorized Version has long been considered the gold standard of biblical diction and has had an incalculable effect on English language and letters, it is not without its detractors. The Pilgrims, for instance, wanted nothing to do with it. And as recently as 1995, the American academic Everett Fox, taking his cue from a closely literal German translation by Martin Buber and Franz Rosenzweig, explicitly rejected King James's verbal riches and produced a text directly based on the Hebrew. Hewing closely to the foreign syntax, Fox's translation favors exact word-for-word correspondences over the modern

Anglophone reader's enjoyment, challenging us "to rethink what these ancient books are and what they mean." He also eschews such "old friends" as Eve's apple, or even the names Eve, Adam, and God (here called "YHWH"). Witness his version of the Tower of Babel (or "Bavel/Babble") story: "Now all the earth was of one language and one set-of-words. ... They said, each man to his neighbor: Come-now! Let us bake bricks and let us burn them well-burnt!"[8] On one level, Fox's conceit is laudable, especially with regard to a work so familiar as to be taken for granted. But in consciously eschewing the seductions of mellifluent prose, he subverts a primary aim of the Bible, as of any manifesto: to attract adherents. Strictly as prose, Fox's Bible walks a fine line between intellectual challenge and distracting awkwardness, and all too often loses its balance. It's as if we were being asked to experience God's scrambling of human language even as we read about it.

The Babel episode, needless to say, is hardly an innocent choice, and can be said to frame the entire translation debate. For God's scattering of languages and peoples "over the face of all the earth," while it effectively closes humanity's doorway to the divine, simultaneously opens the window to a flowering of linguistic and cultural diversity that helps make life here-below worth living, allowing for an otherwise inconceivable circulation of ideas and sounds.

At the opposite end of the spectrum from Everett Fox stands Eugene A. Nida. Though considered one of the most respected authorities in Bible translation, Nida was not himself a translator but rather a consultant to the United Bible Societies, overseeing translations into a variety of languages and cultures in the second half of the twentieth century—a period when, perhaps not coincidentally, the output of Bible translations skyrocketed. Since "no two languages are identical," Nida concluded that "there can be no absolute correspondence between languages.

Hence, there can be no fully exact translations." Rather, as a missionary, he promoted "dynamic" or "functional" equivalence, which sought to ensure that the message of the Scriptures would reach its intended audience, no matter how alien that audience might be from the culture that generated it. The translator's job was to adjust the verbal form of the translation as needed. For instance, in a land that knows no frost, the expression "white as snow" would be changed to "white as egret feathers"; and the actions of Jesus's disciples spreading leaves and branches along the Messiah's path would have to be reimagined for West Africans, for whom such behavior constitutes a grievous offense. Nida was interested in swaying souls. Like Luther, his aim was to speak directly to the reader, with as little cultural static as possible, even if it meant rewriting the source text to get the point across.[9]

Despite the seeming contradictions, we might nonetheless say that Nida, through radically different means, was pursuing an agenda similar to Everett Fox's: addressing his audience—in his case, potential non-Anglophone converts rather than biblical scholars—in the idiom best suited to their concerns. More recently still, the French publisher Bayard sought to bring the Bible to readers of modern fiction, when it commissioned twenty contemporary novelists (among them, Jean Echenoz, Jacques Roubaud, Marie NDiaye, Florence Delay, Emmanuel Carrère, and Valère Novarina) to create a new translation. Working in concert with biblical scholars, the novelists rendered the text into a version that would "confront the literatures of the Bible with contemporary French literatures," in that "successive revolutions in literary and poetic language in the twentieth century have often enabled us to handle the violence, irregularities, occasional absence of formal syntax, and polyphony of the ancient texts."[10] Closely mirroring the Hebrew texts, as did Fox and Rosenzweig, while aiming at an audience raised on literary modernism (as the King James aimed at the contemporary audiences of its time), the Nouvelle traduction joins a tradition that stretches as far back as Saint Jerome, and that continues unabated.

That the Bible continues to exert a linguistic fascination, despite having lost much of its spiritual authority, is due to several facts. For one, unlike secular texts, it is virtually always read in translation: indeed, there is no true original, the source text itself being "a palimpsest of versions in Hebrew, Aramaic, and Greek, along with a vast quantity of commentaries and other religious writings."[11] For another, the version in which one reads or hears the Bible as a child becomes a kind of de facto original, remaining so even when one grows old enough to know better. Finally, because many accept it as the divine Word, by a cognitive disconnect it becomes removed from notions of variant phrasings and external cultures. If there is a text that persistently transcends its own linguistic status, it is the Good Book—read, embraced, and followed even by those who abhor the very notion of multiculturalism and who look upon anything "foreign" with suspicion and contempt. The translator Edith Grossman cites a Southern bumper sticker that captures all the unwitting humor of such an isolationist stance: "If English Was Good Enough for Jesus, It's Good Enough for Me."

***

Translation in the modern, secular sense began in the West around the fourteenth century, as the long-neglected classical tradition gained new currency and humanism came to the fore. The following century saw the first modern treatise devoted to translation per se—and the first known reflection on translation since Jerome—*De interpretatione recta* (The right way to translate; ca. 1424) by the Florentine humanist and statesman

Leonardo Bruni, who is also considered the first modern historian. A translator in his own right, notably of Aristotle, Bruni used his practical experience to promote translations that took into equal account the original's meaning and style, advocating both philological precision and attention to literary effect, while recognizing that complete fidelity was impossible—precepts that haven't varied much in six hundred years.[12]

The next set of guidelines was issued a hundred years later, in *The Way to Translate Well from One Language into Another* (1540) by the French printer and scholar Étienne Dolet. Dissatisfied, as was Bruni, with both the slavish literalness and the freewheeling adaptation that had characterized medieval translations, Dolet identified five key "musts" for any worthy practitioner, which largely echo his Florentine precursor: a perfect understanding of the author's original work, a thorough command of both source and target languages, avoidance of word-for-word transposition ("which demonstrates nothing but the translator's ignorance"), accessible rather than obscure syntax, and a sense of style.[13] All this seems fairly commonsensical and would probably sit well in most translators' laptops even today. Regardless, in 1546 Dolet was found guilty of, again, heresy for a version of Plato that presumably followed these same precepts, and was hanged and burned at the stake, making him, if not translation's first martyr—Tyndale went to the stake ten years earlier—then perhaps the first to be condemned for a secular text. (But hardly the last, as the senseless stabbing of Hitoshi Igarashi, the Japanese translator of Salman Rushdie's *The Satanic Verses*, made all too plain.)

In spite of Dolet's untimely end, the sixteenth century witnessed a flowering of statements on the art of translation, often in the form of the translator's preface to a given work. Many took the opportunity to defend a particular approach or, in time-honored academic fashion, bash their predecessors. Though generally concerned with a specific translation, a number of them, in articulating the principles underlying the text at hand, also laid the groundwork for the more theoretical constructs of later centuries. This flowering did not, however, mean that translation as such was granted higher status. The Cambridge scholar and member of Parliament Thomas Wilson, in his preface to *The Three Orations of Demosthenes* ("Englished out of the Greeke" in 1570), was typical in bemoaning his own inability to convey "the excellence of [the author's] tongue," and offered up translation as a kind of booby prize: "Such as are grieved with translated books, are like to them that eating fine Manchet, are angry with others that feed on Cheate bread. And yet God knoweth men would as gladly eat Manchet as they, if they had it. But all can not wear Velvet, or feed with the best."[14]

Wilson despaired of translation altogether. Others, in the wake of Bruni and Dolet, fretted over how closely to mirror the original. This highly polarizing question soon became a primary focus of translation commentary, and the years following the Renaissance witnessed a great chorus of passionate, eloquent cheering for one team or the other (which by now has swelled into enough views and counterviews and counter-counterviews to fill a massive bookcase).

On the one side, we run across such partisans of free translation as the seventeenth-century poet and critic John Dryden. Himself something of a secular patron saint to translators ("When discussing the poet as translator, from time immemorial it has been the custom to start out by quoting Dryden," is how Kenneth Rexroth started out his own discussion), Dryden is still considered by many the very model of rational good sense, for both his advocacy of empathetic flexibility and his warning to those who would read his prescriptions as license to embroider freely. "A translator that would write with any force or spirit of an original must never dwell on the words of his author," he wrote. "He ought to possess himself entirely and perfectly comprehend the genius and sense of his author. ... And then he will express himself as justly, and with as much life, as if he wrote an original." Trying to produce a word-for-word translation that read well, said Dryden, was like "dancing on ropes with fetter'd legs! A man may shun a fall by using Caution, but the gracefulness of Motion is not to be expected."[15]

In the late eighteenth century, the Scottish writer and jurist Alexander Fraser Tytler nonetheless tried to reconcile "ease with fidelity" by offering three basic principles: that the translation "should give a complete transcript of the ideas of the original," that "the style and manner of writing should be of the same character," and that it "should have all the ease of original composition." In order to realize "this difficult union," the translator "must adopt the very soul of his author, which must speak through his own organs"—which ultimately was not much different from Dryden's "possessing himself entirely."[16]

Others, meanwhile, have taken issue with the very notion of "force or spirit" espoused by Dryden and his kind. Such was the case of the nineteenth-century critic R. H. Horne, who thundered against any departure from strict adherence:

> The only merit ... in a translation is that of giving the words of an author in another language, as nearly by equivalents as possible. ... The instant a man says, "I will give the *spirit* of the author in the words that author would have used had he lived now, and written in this other language," it is all over with the original. Translation, in such a case, becomes a mere cover for individual egotism and vanity.[17]

Horne's remarks fit into a controversy that came to a head in England shortly afterward—and that in many respects suggests the proverbial tempest in a teacup. Still, what gives this particular tempest some force is not only that one can still hear echoes of it in contemporary theory but also that, at least in the Anglophone tradition, it helped lower the status of the translator in ways that make George Eliot's dictum from that same period sound all too current: "A good translator is infinitely below the man who produces *good* original works," she said, though she did allow that he was "above the man who produces *feeble* original works," which was awfully big of her.[18] The fact that Eliot had herself translated Spinoza and Feuerbach makes her dismissal ironic, perhaps, but hardly unique: the Victorian age was notable for producing a surge of translation criticism, some of it quite heated, but it took for granted that translation was a servile genre.

Much of Victorian-era translation was devoted to poetry and the classics, Homer in particular, and it was in fact Homer who occasioned the most renowned debate of the period. Centering on rival versions by Matthew Arnold and Francis William Newman, in its broad lines it did no more than rehash the same old tussle over scholarly fidelity versus poetic effect, yet managed nonetheless to ignite a furore in the literary circles of the day (those wacky Victorians). Newman, a classics professor, was a staunch opponent of the notion that the translation should read like an original: "I aim at precisely the opposite—to retain every peculiarity of the original, so far as I am able, *with the greater care the more foreign it may be.*" (In this, Newman both exposed his academic roots and anticipated the "foreignizing" theories of the late twentieth century.) Arnold, a poet as well as a critic, took care on the other hand "to avoid anything which may the least check or surprise the reader, whom Homer does not check or surprise." The translator, he wrote in one of several rebuttals to Newman, "must without scruple sacrifice, where it is necessary, verbal fidelity to his original, rather than run any risk of producing, by literalness, an odd and unnatural effect." Each, in his way, was striving for a kind of fidelity: Newman, to the form of Homer's language for those who could not read the Greek; Arnold, to the beauties inherent in Homer's expression.[19]

At the same time, while Arnold's position seems the more populist, wittingly or not he helped bolster the perception of translation as something for specialized readers only, a mindset that burdens it still. According to him, the only competent judge of a translation's success was not the translator or the common reader but the scholar conversant in both languages. As such, he denied agency to both the author of the translation, who often draws on instinct and talent to know when something feels right, and the reader, who decides whether or not the translation "speaks" to her—with the logical conclusion that if only scholars can appreciate a translation, then by implication translations are only for scholars. An additional Victorian "tic," of favoring consciously archaized and artificial language in rendering antique texts, pushed translation even further into the realm of minority interest.

Homer, in fact, seems to have given the Bible a run for its money in generating such controversies. In the early 1700s, the classicist Richard Bentley dismissed Alexander Pope's sprightly rendering of the *Iliad*,

> Achilles' wrath, to Greece the direful spring
> Of woes unnumber'd, heav'nly Goddess, sing!

with the oft-quoted putdown "a very pretty poem, Mr. Pope, but you must not call it Homer," then proposed in its place a version so dust-dry that Homer himself would have gagged on it. More than a hundred years later, Dante Gabriel Rossetti defended translators such as Pope on the grounds that "literality of rendering is altogether secondary" and that "a good poem [must] not be turned into a bad one."[20] Yet while Pope's translation, as Rossetti recognized, clearly makes for superior literature, its virtues are not unimpeachable. The criteria of "good" and "bad" not only lie with the beholder but also change with the times. Pope's *Iliad* suited an audience with a taste for flowery language and heroic couplets, but—much as I hate to credit a pedant like Bentley—I would wager that those who still read it today enjoy it less as a representation of Homer than as a prime sample of Pope.

***

Infidelity, exclusion, obsolescence: over the centuries, numerous factors have hindered the mainstream embrace of translation. And one more: the issue of trust, which can stretch from doubts about a literary translator's qualifications all the way to life-threatening suspicions about an interpreter's reliability. The nervous-making reality is that all communication rests on a suspension of disbelief, and, especially in times of war, that suspension can become extremely difficult to uphold. The film *Breaker Morant* (1980), to take one example, shows a Dutch interpreter working with the British during the Boer War being shot dead in the street, partly because he had given false testimony at Morant's court-martial, but also because no one believed he hadn't quietly tipped off the Boers while ostensibly requesting intelligence. As recently as 2011, the *Armed Forces Journal* reported that interpreters in Iraq were "10 times more likely to die in combat than deployed American or international forces,"[21] because neither the troops they were interpreting for nor the enemy they were speaking to had complete confidence in the fidelity of what they were relating. The list is long.

This was not merely—or not always—a matter of paranoia, for the history of translation and that of espionage reveal some telling intersections. Among others, the explorer and linguist Sir Richard Burton, best known for his classic renditions of *One Thousand and One Nights* and the *Kama Sutra*, is also generally acknowledged to have been a spy for the East India Company. And C. K. Scott Moncrieff, whose *Remembrance of Things Past* remains a primary reference for readers of Proust in English, gathered intelligence for the British in Mussolini's Italy in the 1920s. Using as cover his lifestyle as a cosmopolitan aesthete, Scott Moncrieff traveled around Italy—a bit of tourism here, a bit of snooping there—secretly amassing data about the Italian military buildup along the way. His wide circle of friends included bookish Italian aviators, who in the relaxed atmosphere of literary confabs let slip useful tidbits of intel that Scott Moncrieff passed along to the Home Office.[22]

In some ways, translation and spying are natural bedfellows: both involve double allegiances, parallel modes of expression, the ability to observe and interpret; to jump, like a seasoned performer, from one role to another, one voice to another, one persona to another. And, as with a performer, the translator's loyalties are never to be taken for granted. "A translator," writes Bernard Turle, "is a spy whose paymaster is a writer. He is at the service of the latter's principles, themes, discourse, images, his style, image, ego, and he is at the service above all of the implacable imperative *not to betray him*. Yet he is a dandy too: he follows the original text as a dandy follows fashion."[23] In other words, a translator is a double agent, constantly playing two texts, two languages, two cultures, two readerships off each other in order to arrive at a truth that ultimately serves no master but his own exacting ideal of excellence.

Besides, isn't translation by nature a kind of code breaking, the interpretation of one set of significations (informational or stylistic) in terms of another? And hasn't history shown time and again—on the battlefield, in enemy territory, or among the orthodox—that the failure to interpret these significations correctly can entail the loss, not only of your professional reputation, but of your life?

3   Pure Language

While many translators would tell you that their activity is still woefully undervalued, its fortunes began to reverse beginning in the late 1950s, and the past few decades have seen the dramatic rise of the discipline known as "translation studies." Initially slotted in academe as a subhead of literature or linguistics, translation studies has continued to gain traction, and an increasing number of universities offer programs that treat it as a field in its own right. The mainstay of translation studies is, naturally, theoretical statements about the meaning and purpose of translation, and while the core curriculum includes many influential voices, two in particular, both German, have had arguably the greatest roles in shaping current thinking on the topic: Friedrich Schleiermacher and Walter Benjamin.

In his lecture of 1813, "On the Different Methods of Translating," the philosopher and theologian Schleiermacher countered the assertions of Dryden and his followers by denying that the translator's goal should be a smooth-flowing text. In contrast to "the imitator," who "merely wants to produce on the reader an impression similar to that received from the original by its contemporaries," the "genuine translator," argued Schleiermacher,

"wants to bring ... his author and his reader truly together."
Schleiermacher's goal was to lead the reader toward an "understanding of the original language ... the same impression [the
translator] himself has gained [of the work] through his knowledge of the original language." In other words, the translation
should retain features of the original that both underscore its
status as a translation and enlighten the reader about the pecu-
liar properties of the source language by mimicking them as
closely as possible. The more foreign-sounding, the better. By
forcing the target language into unfamiliar contortions based
on the syntax and usage of the original, said Schleiermacher,
the translation invigorates and renews the target's own linguistic resources—for, as Goethe noted not long afterward, "In the
end every literature grows bored if it is not refreshed by foreign
participation."[1]

Schleiermacher was writing in the early nineteenth century,
at a time when German language and culture felt the need for
such refreshment (much as English had been reinvigorated by
its contact with Norman French as of the eleventh century, and
would be again in the twentieth by languages such as Yiddish
and Spanish). More recently, his prescription of "moving the
reader toward the author" has been embraced by proponents of
foreignization, who aim to resist perceived Anglo-American eth-
nocentrism by bending English to the source language's norms,
and who see in Schleiermacher's arguments a counterweight to
the imperialistic, "domesticating" approach of most contemporary translations (more on this later). The irony is that there is
also a nation-building subtext to Schleiermacher's argument that
harks straight back to the Romans—and that, with its historical
imperative of gathering all foreign treasures into the Teutonic
storehouse, rings both idealistic and ominous:

Just as our soil has itself become richer and more fertile and our climate milder and more pleasant only after much transplantation of foreign flora, just so we sense that our language ... can thrive in all its freshness and completely develop its own power only through the most many-sided contacts with what is foreign. And coincidentally our nation may be destined ... to carry all the treasures of foreign art and scholarship, together with its own, in its language, to unite them into a great historical whole, so to speak, which would be preserved in the center and heart of Europe, so that, with the help of our language, whatever beauty the most different times have brought forth can be enjoyed by all people.[2]

A related idealism seems to underwrite Walter Benjamin's oft-cited essay "The Task of the Translator" (1923). Like Schleiermacher, Benjamin rejected the notion that the "highest praise" one can give a translation is "that it reads as if it had originally been written in that language." Rather, a good translation "does not cover the original, does not block its light, but allows the pure language, as though reinforced by its own medium, to shine upon the original all the more fully. This may be achieved, above all, by a literal rendering of the syntax. ... It is the task of the translator to release in his own language that pure language which is ... imprisoned in a work."[3] By releasing this idealized language, which exists somewhere between source and target, the translator lifts the source work into a "higher and purer linguistic air," in which its "afterlife," its continued survival, becomes possible.

Benjamin's essay has become a standard reference for students of translation, and it offers much to ponder. For one thing, he challenges the received notion that translation is about the transmission of meaning. Likening it to reassembly of the fragments of a shattered vessel, he argues that "a translation, instead of resembling the meaning of the original, must lovingly and in detail incorporate the original's mode of signification, thus making both the original and the translation recognizable as fragments of a greater language." This "greater" or "pure" language, "which no longer means or expresses anything," reveals the "kinship of languages" that rests "in the intention underlying each language as a whole ... which no single language can attain by itself."

Still, for all its idealization of the translator's task, Benjamin's essay perpetuates the qualitative dichotomy between the original and its shadow; for while the poet's intention is "spontaneous, primary, graphic," the translator's is "derivative, ultimate, ideational," and by inference, secondary. Moreover, while the original offers a unity of content and language, "like a fruit and its skin," the translation merely enfolds the content without melding the two. It is always outside looking in, rather than a participant in its own significant creation.

Because translation is seen as derivative and abstract, its ultimate merit in Benjamin's view is not to produce a new literary work, but rather to have "extended the boundaries of the German language," the same case that Schleiermacher made for it in the previous century. We might argue that the translator's real task, in this day and age, is to enhance a given culture's offerings by introducing riches imported from elsewhere and allowing its citizens—its readers—to share in them. But Benjamin shuts down any such considerations at the outset: "In the appreciation of a work of art or an art form, consideration of the receiver never proves fruitful. ... No poem is intended for the reader, no picture for the beholder, no symphony for the listener." Consequently, "whenever a translation undertakes to serve the reader," it is by nature a failure. Translation, breathing of a "higher and purer linguistic air," instead points the way toward, but never reaches, the "inaccessible realm of reconciliation and fulfillment of all languages." It's an enticing theoretical construct, much like Stéphane Mallarmé's quintessential Book to end all books, or André Breton's "point of the mind at which life and death, the real and the imagined, past and future, the communicable and the incommunicable, high and low, cease to be perceived as contradictions."[4] But, devoid of human presence and disdainful of human response, it exists only in the most rarefied atmosphere, unconnected to real linguistic exchange, and its end point might be not so much pure as sterile.

***

On a practical level, one drawback of both Schleiermacher's "genuine" translation and Benjamin's "pure language" is that they can easily be taken for what the translation theorist André Lefevere calls a "very spirited defense of what we now know as 'translationese,' " and their products virtually indistinguishable from merely clunky attempts at English. Alongside this, their joint legacy is a shift in translation theory away from praxis and toward a more formalist, linguistics-and-mathematics-derived approach (replete with diagrams and x- and y-axes) that tries to reduce translation strategies to a defined set of immutable, quantifiable laws. As translation studies moves from being what the translation theorist James S. Holmes labeled "an underdeveloped country in the world of literary scholarship" toward nationhood of its own, we find more and more statements along the lines of this pseudoscientific babble, also by the much-venerated Holmes: "It is clear that the repertory must not only be quite complete, but also complex enough in structure to accommodate a number of parametric axes. Among these a major one, of course, is the axis microstructure-mesostructure-macrostructure (from grapheme/morpheme via lexeme, sentence, and suprasentential units to text) …"[5]

In part, this is a predictable effect of academia, in which theory, the more abstruse the better, becomes its own justification—particularly since many authors of such theories are not themselves practicing translators. It might seem like a classic instance of "those who can't do, teach," but it's more complicated than that. There is, admittedly, an intellectual thrill to taking ideas and twisting them around into new shapes— translating them, as it were, into new ideas—which is no less seductive than the act of writing itself. It is also true that most translation practice, as well as a lot of older translation theory, has a commonsense, tried-and-true quality to it that simply isn't very sexy, and that doesn't provide much grist for the kinds of hotly debated papers at ALA or ALTA conferences on which academic reputations are built.

Don't get me wrong: I value theoretical scholarship, especially unorthodox, all the more so when it forces me to question my own assumptions. The problem is, much of the translation theory emerging from academe is simply of little use in either helping anyone understand what translation is, or, from a practical standpoint, helping produce better translations. While the theoretical statements of earlier centuries generally aimed at defending or attacking a given approach, current studies focus on a much more notional variety of the subject. The result is a widening breach between translation as an art or craft and a discourse that tends to push it increasingly into the realm of impracticability. Translation theory is one of the few disciplines in which the study of a subject seems bent on demonstrating that very subject's futility.

In fact, there are those for whom the futility of translation, and its imminent demise, are a fait accompli. The poet-provocateur Kenneth Goldsmith, in a brief diatribe called *Against*

Translation: Displacement Is the New Translation (published in an eight-language boxed set), contrasts translation proper—"the ultimate humanist gesture ... an overly cautious bridge builder ... a boutique pursuit from a lost world"—with displacement, aka appropriation: "rude and insistent," a "brutal fact," and the only valid means of transferring a text from one understanding to another in the contemporary context. Why the only valid means? Because language, Goldsmith quotes John Cage as saying, is by nature a militaristic structure, "the arrangement of the army," thus "ripe for contestation." Echoes Goldsmith: "Question linguistic structures, question political structures."[6] In other words, rather than wasting time on issues like fidelity or foreignization, find more and more texts to drop into strange surroundings. All of which is perfectly valid and a little so-what.

I'll admit that, as a translator with both feet planted on the side of praxis, I have scant patience with tortured theoretical blockades, or with clever slogans that are easy to shout but harder to make meaningful, or with convoluted formulations seemingly designed mainly to tickle the fancies of grad students. Just as teaching someone about composition and plotting does not produce a great author, so theories of translation will not produce better translators. *That* part happens in the smithy of our souls, as Joyce had it—in the empathy we can feel for what we're translating, in the resources we can dredge out of our own linguistic capabilities, in the instincts we can marshal when choosing exactly how to convey a particular blend of tone, sense, sensibility, music, information, emotion, and rhythm.

That said, the serious interrogation of the subject over the last half-century (even if in order to find it one has to wash away vast quantities of silt) indicates a salutary evolution in attitudes toward translation as a discipline worthy of attention and study, something not to be undertaken lightly and to be accorded the same respect as other literary disciplines. Perhaps more important, the concerns raised by modern translation theory, in matters of cultural appropriation, gender studies, and postcolonial politics, just might force us to question the underlying assumptions of translation as a practice—in a real way, not a glib Goldsmithy way—and revivify it, restoring to it something it has often lacked: an ethical dimension, by which I mean a *human* dimension.

***

The increasingly abstract strain of scholarly translation theory has had an even less human parallel in the industrial world. The ultimate in Augustinian conformity, machine translation (MT) eschews all notion of idiosyncrasy or personal creativity in favor of a more systematized, normative process, in which efficiency and accuracy are the goal. Although MT remains an imperfect tool at best and is used mainly for nonliterary forms of translation, it's not inconceivable that as artificial intelligence matures, more sophisticated algorithms could enable it to make the kinds of distinctions on which literary translations depend.

The dream of self-generating translation is an old one, and it goes hand in hand with such Babel-reversing universal languages as Johann Martin Schleyer's Volapük (1879) and Ludwik Zamenhof's Esperanto (1887), and before them, the attempts at a universal grammar by Leibnitz and others. Devices to facilitate translation were initially conceived as aids to simultaneous interpretation—the first patent for one, based on an idea by the Boston department-store tycoon Edward Filene and known as the Filene-Finlay Speech Translator, was taken out in 1926—and gained prominence in 1945, with the first use of machine-assisted interpretation at the Nuremberg Trials. The devices used were notable because they offered four languages simultaneously (English, French, Russian, and German), something that had never been done before, but they still relied on human translators speaking their interpretations into a telephone-like receiver.[7]

Machine-assisted translation in the current sense was inspired by the work of the English code breakers at Bletchley Park during World War II, and was founded on the belief that language was itself a kind of code to be deciphered—once again, the translator as cryptographer, as spy. Warren Weaver, a vice president of the Rockefeller Foundation, whose 1949 memorandum is credited with launching the first wave of research into MT, expressed as much when he wrote, "When I look at an article in Russian, I say: 'This is really written in English, but it has been coded in some strange symbols. I will now proceed to decode.' "[8] In his view of languages as interchangeable systems, Weaver echoes Benjamin's notion of the "kinship of languages," and the earliest machines seemed to bear him out: inevitably crude, they were nonetheless promising enough to unleash a flood of government funding and rampant optimism about the imminent reality of fully automated translation. By the late 1950s, however, the complexities of how language actually works had begun to manifest in highly disappointing data.

The problem, of course, is that software is literal while language is not. Words do not always have direct equivalents in other languages, and even when they do, they're not always consistent. The contextual shadings that can cause an identical semantic structure to mean very different things are instinctively perceived by the human brain, but they are often undetectable to the artificial one. How can you teach a computer, for example, to distinguish among the different functions of the suffix *-er* in the words *pager*, *paler*, and *paper*? Or decide whether, in the phrase "check tires for wear and damage," the word *damage* is a noun or a verb? Or determine whether the sentence "He ran the man down" means catching up with him, tiring him out, or hitting him with a car? As research continued and examples proliferated, the quality of the resulting translations sharply declined, and enthusiasm for MT dwindled.[9]

Research in recent decades has revived interest, as the development of digital technology has allowed for more refined distinctions; but even today, computers often require human assistance. In my own experience, I once worked on a business translation project that involved editing a voluminous computer-generated draft. Combing through the mass of output, I routinely encountered such non sequiturs as "nails, screws, hinges, strawberries ..."—with *fraise* rendered not as "drill bit," as the passage required, but as the more common "strawberry"— making me wonder whether it wouldn't have been faster and more efficient to translate from scratch. Naturally, in the "that was then, this is now" world of technology, we can expect that computers will eventually learn to distinguish between soft fruit and hardware. But in the near term, at least, some form of human post-editing seems required.

In addition, MT is still mainly intended for utilitarian forms of translation, such as business and technical documents or news reports. The more one moves away from translation as equivalence and paraphrase—that is, the more one enters the domain of literature, with its myriad shadings, neologisms, and ambiguities—the less applicable MT becomes, as even its boosters freely recognize. "The purpose of machine translation," writes one group of authors, "is, on the one hand, to relieve the human translator of the need to work with tedious, repetitive and aesthetically unsatisfying material and, on the other, to speed up and facilitate worldwide information dissemination. ... Translating fiction and poetry is not a task for machine translation."[10]

Not everyone has wanted to limit the machines to such functional chores, however: In the 1950s, the linguist Anthony G. Oettinger, in a paper forbiddingly titled "Automatic (Transference, Translation, Remittance, Shunting)," predicted that computers would eventually relieve translators of their "tedious routine manual and mental labors," and trumpeted the "mass-production ... assembly line" benefits of such an approach. Oettinger was not speaking merely of technical or business translation, for the type of program he envisioned, alert to polysemy, could also handle the multiple meanings beloved by human novelists and poets. Whenever it encountered a polysemous word, the computer would group its possible translations in parentheses (as in Oettinger's title) for the human operator to choose between. "An editor presented with the original text [of a novel] and a translated version prepared by an automatic dictionary would be free to devote his attention to historical and literary context, to nuance, to style," Oettinger exults, as if nuance and style were mere frills. "It would remain only to select, combine, and season to taste."[11] Translation Helper—just add water.

As anyone who has edited a translation knows, "seasoning" is the least of our concerns. Revising a translation, like the work of translation itself, involves evaluation and a large helping of human instinct—at least if we wish to avoid the kinds of pitfalls that are the hallmarks of bad translation. This becomes especially clear to anyone who has tried running a literary text through

Google Translate. The friend of travelers everywhere, Google is perfect for explaining to a Czech pharmacist that you need aspirin or for giving you the gist of a foreign-language website, but is uneven at best when dealing with belles lettres. It's important to remember that Google is a search engine, not a translation program per se; it works not by generating new translations but by accessing the vast corpus of previously existing translations floating in the ether. In theory, this means that the more popular a literary passage, and the more available it is online, the more likely Google will "produce" an accurate translation of it. But even here, results vary. Thus, for example, Proust's famous opening sentence, "Longtemps je me suis couché de bonne heure," is translated by Google as "For a long time I went to bed early," virtually a word-for-word reproduction of the Scott Moncrieff translation; but Camus's equally famous incipit, "Aujourd'hui maman est morte," comes out "Today, my mother is dead," which, though reasonably accurate, diverges both from Stuart Gilbert's standard English version, "Mother died today," and from the author's intent. Running more complicated, and less famous, quotes through Google yields a predictable patchwork of accurate phrases, unnatural syntax, and gibberish that sounds like the user's guide to a foreign-made appliance.[12]

Perhaps these problems will fade as the technology improves, or perhaps the constantly evolving quirks of usage and lexicon in a living language will always elude the capacities of even the nimblest electronic brains. For now, we fossils who harbor a quaint fondness for notions such as individual style can take heart from the fact that, when it comes to literature—as opposed to, say, chess, with its mathematically calculable rules and options—computers will have a hard time keeping up with humans for at least a little while longer. On that score, the most encouraging bit of evidence that language hasn't entirely been purified, and the one that should be pinned to every human translator's bulletin board, is the attempt by a Russian computer some years ago to render the English saying "The spirit is willing but the flesh is weak." With mechanical aplomb, it spat out what to its circuits must have seemed a perfectly sound analogue: "The vodka is strong, but the meat is rotten."[13]

4 Beautifully Unfaithful

It was the seventeenth-century French critic Gilles Ménage who coined the term *les belles infidèles* (the beautiful, unfaithful ones), after a venerably sexist French adage likening translations to women, in that they can be comely or faithful but never both. Ménage's quip referred to the reigning tendency in French-language translation at the time, as exemplified by the translator Nicolas Perrot d'Ablancourt, to "update" the ancient Greek and Latin texts—that is, to remove vulgar language or sexual references, as well as to transpose things like currency and honorifics into their modern French counterparts—in order to fit prevailing standards of easy comprehensibility and *bon ton*. The translations were "beautiful," in that they read smoothly and flattered consumer expectations, but faithful in the strict sense they were not. The fact that this tendency was sufficiently widespread and long-lasting to be known ever after as the "*belles infidèles* approach" does not mean that it was an especially notable phenomenon; indeed, the terms of the debate between beauty and fidelity remain more or less as they were when it began, some two thousand years ago.

One reason for this longevity is that no one has been able to define, once and for all, exactly what *fidelity* means in the context of translation. John Dryden grumbled that the original author "can turn and vary [his thoughts] as he pleases, till he renders them harmonious; but the wretched translator has no such privilege [and] must make what music he can in the expression." The scholar Michael Hanne takes a more positive view, arguing that "only a beautiful translation can be truly faithful to a fine original." Edith Grossman cautions that "fidelity should never be confused with literalness." Umberto Eco, as an author, considered the translation faithful when "the English text says exactly what I wanted to say," regardless of whether it diverges from the Italian. And, according to Grossman, Borges went even further, recommending that all the polysyllabic words in his Spanish original be replaced in translation by good, sharp, Anglo-Saxon monosyllables: "Simplify me," he prescribed. "Make me stark. My language often embarrasses me. It's too youthful, too Latinate. ... Make me macho and gaucho and skinny."[1]

What the concordant but inconclusive nature of these prescriptions suggests above all is that the ways in which they can be enacted change with the circumstances, and that there are no definitive answers. Texts are read for many reasons, and one is "faithful" to different originals via different paths. You might successfully convey the atmosphere of a haiku or the humor of a comic strip by playing fast and loose, but as Bible translation in the Renaissance demonstrated, not striking the right balance between style and accuracy can sometimes get you burnt well-burnt at the stake.

Proponents of literalism argue that a benefit of preserving the foreignness of the foreign and bringing the reader to the author is that you move readers out of their familiar space and into somewhere new (though one could argue that all good literature does this, regardless of origin). Taking this to extremes leaves one with something akin to Mark Twain's parodic back-translation from the French of one of his own stories: "It there was one time here an individual known under the name of Jim Smiley ...".[2] Less radically, it entails preserving specific cultural references that remind the reader of the work's alien status. An old French ad for Menier chocolate shows a child scrawling the words *Evitez les contrefaçons*, which we could translate either as *Avoid imitations,* or else as the more familiar *Accept no substitutes.* One translation gives us a glimpse of how the French think, the other "moves the text toward the reader" by phrasing it the way the same ad in English might phrase it. Which is the more faithful?

Similarly, the translator Lawrence Venuti criticizes William Weaver, in his 1968 translation of Italo Calvino's *Cosmicomics,* for replacing the original *tagliatelle* with *noodles,* arguing that the specificity and Italianness of *tagliatelle* gives the work a particular character that is erased in English.[3] But we could just as easily defend Weaver for using a term that was familiar to his American readers in the same way that *tagliatelle* was to Italians, thereby maintaining the effect of the text and not forcing Anglophones to puzzle over something that Italians would have taken for granted. Moreover, language and usage change: *tagliatelle,* presumably considered too exotic fifty years ago, is now commonly recognized here.

Needless to say, a solid understanding of and sympathy with the source culture and language is key—otherwise, you might end up completely mistaking the connotations of *tagliatelle,* or, to borrow an illustration from Nabokov, translating the phrase *bien-être général* not as *overall well-being* but as the howler *it's good to be a general.* The translator Judson Rosengrant argues that "fine translation" is "both scholarship and art, each reinforcing

the other," which is a fine ideal. At the same time, solid understanding does not in itself guarantee a felicitous translation, and
sometimes can stand in its way by making every available option
seem hopelessly inadequate.

Even more than the ability to seize every nuance of the
source, I would argue that the single most crucial requirement
in producing a viable target version is to be a talented writer in
one's own language. We could fill barrels (to be then rolled off
cliffs) with scholars who can identify every hue and shade of a
foreign text, yet lack the stylistic facility in their own to re-create
these subtleties. "All the worst translations are done by experts
in the foreign language who know little or nothing about the
poetry alongside which their translations will be read," protests
Peter Cole. "Foreign-language academics are largely concerned
with semantical accuracy, rendering supposedly exact meanings
into a frequently colorless or awkward version of the translation
language." It's not only about scholarly equivalences, it's also
about linguistic ambiance. Though a number of translators have
chosen to live abroad, for me it seems essential to be surrounded
by my target language, the better to stay current with the changing colors and tonalities of its usage. Asked if his Spanish was
good enough to translate García Márquez's *One Hundred Years of
Solitude*, Gregory Rabassa shrewdly replied that the real question
was whether his *English* was good enough.[4]

If translation is assumed to be *in the service* of the source text,
a hunt for elusive equivalences, then it is doomed to be judged
negatively—at best, to paraphrase Beckett, by how well it fails.
But once we see the translation as a creative work in its own right,
one that conveys the essence, spirit, and, to the extent possible,
form of someone else's text while communicating a literary pleasure all its own, then it becomes less an impossible pursuit and

more (to borrow Ralph Manheim's formulation) a performance to be appraised on its own merits. Rather than *equivalence*, or the other terms commonly employed—*re-creation, identity, analogy, match*—I would use the word *representation*. A good translation offers not a reproduction of the work but an interpretation, a re-presentation, just as the performance of a play or a sonata is a representation of the script or the score, one among many possible representations. I think of it as analogous to a good cover version of a favorite song, one that might not sound like the original but that finds the essence of the song and re-creates it differently; that makes the listener hear the song in a way that both preserves and renews it. Moreover, I would take issue with Franz Rosenzweig's well-known definition of the translator's lot as "to serve two masters," the foreign work and the target reader. Translators have a distinct responsibility toward the text and toward the reader, but they do not serve. Rather, they create something new, something that does not diminish the original work but rather adds something of value to the sum total of global literatures.

The question, as always, is whether the text produces the desired effect, to which the answer is, ultimately, subjective: a translator must first interpret the original, see what effect it has on her, and then try to represent that effect in a language and culture not the author's own. Whether that original will have the same effect on other readers is anyone's guess. Whether each subsequent reading will always have the same effect even on the translator is indeterminate. But to the best of their abilities and judgment, good translators produce versions that re-create the complex web of responses that they as readers have had to the source text, versions that will establish a setting liable to elicit those responses in others.

As we have seen time and again, *faithful* is an endlessly debatable term, so malleable and polyvalent as to finally become meaningless. A translation has to represent the original in a way that allows a target reader to experience as much as possible the spirit and purpose and pleasure (or distaste) and vigor (or indolence) of the work on which it's based. It has to speak to the reader in a way that justifies the original's claim of being worthy of translation to begin with. It has to be *convincing*.

***

Although literary translation might not bear the immediate repercussions of, say, the simultaneous interpretation of a UN policy address or a bilingual medical consult, it nonetheless entails certain issues that carry deep political and ethical implications. Dating back at least as far as the Romans and their appropriation of Greek oratory, these issues remain no less relevant to our contemporary concerns with cultural hegemony and empowerment.

What is the translator's responsibility, and how best to actualize it? The answer boils down to two not-so-simple words: *respect* and *empathy*. Respect for the work one is translating, for the place—in both the geographical and psychological sense—from which it comes, as well as for one's own labor as a translator and for the reader who will eventually consume the fruits of that labor. Empathy for the intent behind the written artifact. Constance Garnett asserted that a translator's primary qualifications were "to be in sympathy with the author he is translating" and "to be in love with words" and all their meanings: "The language of a country is the soul of the people, and if you debase the language you debase the people and rob them of their heritage."[5]

This does not mean setting aside our judgment or ability to intervene. We want to do right by our authors, dead or alive, and sometimes that means using our attunement to the text to know when to keep aspects of it from interfering with the reading experience. Respect should never tip into awe, for then it becomes paralyzing. "Just as writing is an act of hubris," writes the translator Burton Raffel, "so too is good translation. The translator cannot afford to be any more modest than the original author was."[6] The wages of too much respect are mediocrity.

That said, and as history has repeatedly shown, it is possible, even in the name of that respect, to enlist translation as a foot soldier in imperial campaigns of cultural expansion. Saint Jerome, the early proponent of liberalism in translation, nonetheless believed that "the translator considers thought content a prisoner which he transplants into his own language with the prerogative of a conqueror."[7] Even now, when we acknowledge Shakespeare's debt to Golding's Ovid, or Keats's to Chapman's Homer, or George Bernard Shaw's (or Katherine Mansfield's, or Raymond Carver's) to Garnett's Chekhov, we may intend to honor the original, but we're really emphasizing its benefit to our language.

To some extent one is tempted to say, with a Gallic shrug, *et alors*? There's nothing inherently wrong with diversifying one's culture—indeed, as Goethe and Schleiermacher recognized, without such dynamic interchanges, languages wither and die (which is why the normalizing efforts of bodies such as the Académie Française seem so vain). Moreover, to the degree that it promotes cross-cultural understanding, translation can help make the alien Other less alien, help advance useful dialogue rather than the border-caulking discourse of hidebound protectionists. Susan Sontag astutely remarked that translation is by nature "an ethical task, and one that mirrors and duplicates the role of literature itself, which is to extend our sympathies ... to secure and deepen the awareness (with all its consequences) that other people, people different from us, really do exist."[8]

As to how those different people become aware of other cultures, it largely depends on where one stands in the linguistic food chain. Translation theorists speak of "vertical" and "horizontal" translation. The first designates translations from a "major" source into a "minor" or "vernacular" target (such as, today, Spanish into Catalan, or, in medieval times, Latin into pretty much anything); the second, translations between two languages of equal prominence. It is especially vertical translation that is at issue in cases of cultural enhancement, such as the Romans borrowing from the Greeks, the French taking from the Italians in the Renaissance, or the Germans amassing "all the treasures of foreign art and scholarship" in Schleiermacher's nineteenth-century scenario (see chapter 3). Paving more of a two-way street, David Bellos speaks of translations "up" or "down," the former taking place when, say, the Icelandic Nobel laureate Halldor Laxness is picked up by Random House; the latter when the Icelandic publisher Bjartur takes on *Harry Potter*. Again, there seems nothing inherently wrong with this, and examples abound of authors (including several listed at the beginning of this book) writing in less frequented languages who have reaped intellectual and financial rewards and attained international prominence from being translated "up," having their works thrust into global languages and markets.

But probing deeper, we find a more sinister side to the process. As the translation scholar Emily Apter notes, translation, while facilitating exchange, can simultaneously act as an "agent of language extinction," condemning "minority tongues to obsolescence, even as it fosters access to the cultural heritage of 'small' literatures."[9] In other words, in a kind of "damned if you do, damned if you don't" quandary, the more that languages like English, Russian, or Chinese gain market share, partly through absorbing the productions of minority cultures like so many corporate acquisitions, the more these minority productions are threatened with irrelevance, forced to push their way onto the world stage via translation (which ultimately redefines and reshapes them) or else fall off the grid entirely. One need only think of the Celtic languages and the honorable though perhaps futile attempts to preserve them. Increasingly, the literature and folklore of such languages live on only through translation into mainstream tongues, while the original versions slowly die out or, as with Sanskrit, become the exclusive province of the erudite. It's a curious paradox, one that highlights the ability of translation not only to unite but also to appropriate. Translation becomes both the bridge linking civilizations and a measure—even an aggravator—of the gulf separating them.

What, you might ask, does all this have to do with the process of ferrying a work between linguistic shores? The answer is that our ever more interconnected societies demand unprecedented attention to the benefits of, and the ethical challenges raised by, cross-cultural and cross-linguistic communication. "In a world where individual nation-states are increasingly enmeshed in financial and information networks, where multiple linguistic and national identities can inhabit a single state's borders or exceed them in vast diasporas, where globalization has its serious—and often violent—discontents, and where terrorism and war transform distrust into destruction, language and translation play central, if often unacknowledged, roles,"[10] writes Sandra Bermann. Otherwise put, translation has become too serious a business to be left to dusty pedants and poets pondering their Chapman.

In response to this quandary and its global implications, current generations of academic theorists have revived the Punic War between fidelity and felicity in a meaner, harsher, more politicized form. For many of these theorists, translation into major Western languages constitutes an act of aggression against the language and culture being translated. Indeed, some theories give rise to the curious phenomenon of the self-hating translator, an odd hybrid who bemoans the fact that his labors aren't sufficiently appreciated yet despises his inescapable role in promoting the marginalization of other cultures. "Reading late twentieth- or twenty-first-century translation theory," quips the (practicing) translator Peter Cole, "one often gets the sense that many of the principal theorists simply resent the imagination, if not the English language itself."[11]

Some of these academics champion "foreignizing" translations that intentionally flout the conventions of the target language to retain those of the source. Taking his cue from the French theorist Antoine Berman, the translator and professor Lawrence Venuti, one of the more outspoken advocates of this method, attacks the notion of fluency in translation as "a discursive sleight of hand" that imposes on the work such "English-language" values as "easy readability, transparent discourse, and the illusion of authorial presence."[12] In Venuti's telling, the literary translator comes off as a kind of CIA wet boy, perpetrating a terrorist act whose "violence ... resides in the very purpose and activity of translation: the reconstitution of the foreign text in accordance with values, beliefs and representations that pre-exist it in the target language ... [which constitutes] an appropriation of foreign cultures for domestic agendas." In his book *The Translator's Invisibility*, he argues for an approach that accentuates the strangeness of the foreign text in its very translation, doing "right abroad" by doing "wrong at home, deviating enough from native norms to stage an alien reading experience."

Venuti's basic point is that translation must not be used to homogenize other cultural viewpoints, and that the "illusion of transparency" resulting from current practice obscures the culturally weighted contribution of the translator. To some extent, this critique is fair enough: there *is* something queasy-making about having to pledge allegiance to a language or culture that aggressively asserts its will to primacy, its desire to exclude those who won't get with the lingo; and many translators (myself included) do seek to create a reader-friendly experience in the target language. But as with many polemics, Venuti's wilts under its own heat. *Of course* translation is a product of interpretative choices conditioned by the translator's home culture. The problem, however, lies not with fluid or intelligible translations per se, but rather with ones that actively pretend they aren't translations at all, or that make changes dictated solely and arbitrarily by the translator's (or publisher's, or audience's) own biases when these are at odds with what the author wrote. Besides, the foreignness of the source text resides not only in its syntax but also in the concerns, viewpoints, settings, and context that its author puts forth, their nonnative character shining almost inevitably through the target version as if through a translucent cloth. Something of the original always seeps into the translation, whether the author's native sensibility, trace elements of the source syntax, or the way the source language helps structure the author's world-view. No matter how fluid in English, would anyone mistake Kafka, or Kundera, for an American writer? There is a large middle ground between "naturalizing" a work so drastically that it becomes denatured and preserving its foreign flavor to the point of serving up gibberish. Imagining the sort of translation Venuti seems to favor, one can't help recalling the *New Yorker* cartoon in which a visibly woebegone translator asks his seething author, "Do you not be happy with me as the translator of the books of you?" (The irony is that Venuti's own translations tend to read with at least reasonable fluency, further pointing to the academic gap between theory and practice.)

Let's be clear: I am not advocating that a translation "normalize" or try to ignore the foreignness of the source text. I'm merely observing that a little foreignization can go a very long way. Ralph Parker, the English translator of Aleksandr Solzhenitsyn's *One Day in the Life of Ivan Denisovich*, added a short but potent four-letter word to English by adapting the author's Russian term for the camp inmates into the highly evocative *zeks*, much as Anthony Burgess reverse-engineered Russian words— *khorosho* ("good") into *horrorshow*—to pepper his droogs' patois in *A Clockwork Orange* and give the book its particular sound. Touches such as these—grace notes rather than full-on crescendos—allow us to appreciate what's foreign about the inspiration without forcing us into an unnecessarily alienating and off-putting reading experience. Moreover, as Bellos notes, the deployment of strange-sounding phrases or syntax to convey the text's nonnative origins is ultimately self-defeating, as such translations will simply be "disregarded as clumsy, awkward, or incomplete," or else, as in the case of *tagliatelle*, what was once a foreignism will simply become part of the target language, no longer foreignizing at all.[13]

To this I would add, as a strategic matter, that in a cultural climate already dismissive of foreign outlooks and literatures, intentionally making them even harder to access seems a classic case of shooting oneself in the foot with a howitzer. As Edith

Grossman points out, "A mindless, literalist translation would constitute a serious breach of contract. There isn't a self-respecting publisher in the world who would not reject a manuscript framed in this way."[14] Despite what Venuti asserts, a good translator aims not to promote some illusory invisibility but rather to infuse the text with an *appropriate* amount of his own personality, gauged on a case-by-case, instance-by-instance basis: enough to give the translation distinction without smothering the original.

It's true that history is filled with examples of translators who have brought their cultural prejudices heavily to bear, as evidenced by the *belles infidèles*. Sometimes the work has suffered for it, as when in the eighteenth century Alexander Tytler (the same Tytler who prescribed a "complete transcript of the ideas of the original") expunged all references to physicality from Homer because they offended "correct taste"; or when J. H. Frere, in the nineteenth century, discarded the "lines of extreme grossness" he found in Aristophanes.[15] (And while we're at it, let's not lose sight of how our own prejudices continue to operate, such as in suppressing language now deemed politically incorrect.) But sometimes these prejudices have yielded idiosyncratic gems, such as the King James Bible, or Ezra Pound's translations of Chinese, Classical, and Provençal poetry, or Edward FitzGerald's *Rubáiyát of Omar Khayyám*.

FitzGerald provides an illuminating example. Castigated by historians of translation for the wide detours he took in rendering the Persian poems of the *Rubáiyát*, he further compounded his case with such culturally arrogant reflections as: "It is an amusement to me to take what Liberties I like with these Persians, who (as I think) are not Poets enough to frighten one from such excursions, and who really do want a little Art to shape them."[16] While I can't endorse his viewpoint, I note that he nonetheless produced a translation of these poems that introduced them to, and still resonates with, a large reading public, whereas later, more culturally sensitive versions have fallen into oblivion.

Moreover, FitzGerald's pronouncement sounds less smug when set alongside another of his credos: "To keep Life in the Work (as Drama must) the Translator (however inferior to his Original) must re-cast that original into his own Likeness, more or less: the less like his original, so much the worse: but still, the live Dog better than the dead Lion."[17] In other words, and yet again, a translation endowed with the breath of life should be considered an independent creation, to be read on its own merits, rather than the pale shadow or exegesis of another work.

But the question remains: Does domestication into one's own culture necessarily mean eradicating the otherness of the original? The examples I've just cited certainly bespeak a desire to boil the foreign text down into something more palatable to homegrown tastes. But I believe that one *can* make a literary work accessible in one's own land while safeguarding its cultural differences. The aim, in other words, is not "to bring back a cultural other as the same, the recognizable, even the familiar,"[18] as Venuti would have it, but to bring back that otherness in ways that make it available to those who could not otherwise benefit. When I try to convey the fluidity and smoothness of Patrick Modiano's French in equally fluid English, it's *his* fluidity I'm seeking to represent, not some hypothetical fluidity of the English language as a whole. Nor does my English version obscure the fact that Modiano's prose reflects a fundamentally non-American sensibility, or that his characters are interacting with foreign settings in ways that an American, even an expatriate one, would not. To my mind, this otherness is a key element of Modiano's work, and making it appreciable to American readers does not, should not, in any way negate it. My goal, then, is to offer readers the best likeness of the work that I can, retaining the quirks and personality of the original, but also making sure my version affords literary enjoyment *in English*—even if that involves a certain creative license. This does not mean trampling heedlessly over the foreign author's work, imposing my own preferences or shoehorning it into my culture's values. At the same time, it also doesn't mean bending and twisting the translation to fit the latest political fashions, or rigidly following a given theoretical approach. What it does mean is being sufficiently attuned to each nuance to divine where the author was going, and knowing when to follow closely and when to deviate a bit in order to arrive at the same destination. It means constantly interrogating the text, trying to get behind it and adapting when necessary.

On this score, different translators have found their comfort zone at different points along the spectrum. My usual position is to let the inherent foreignness of the author's viewpoint seep through prose that, in other respects, is no stranger in English (but also no less strange) than it would be in French. But even then, it's a tricky balance, often decided on a case-by-case basis, and by feel rather than hard-and-fast rule. I probably wouldn't call a character named François "Frank," but neither would I have him exclaim "Mon dieu!" as if in a bad Maurice Chevalier movie. Bellos takes matters a quarter step further by leaving certain terms (interjections, official titles, foodstuffs) in the original. On the flip side of the coin, the British translator of Frédéric Beigbeder's novel *99 francs*, in an update of the *belles infidèles*, transposed the author's trendy Parisian hotspots into more familiar London ones, and the title into the Brit-friendly *£9.99* (the Spanish version, meanwhile, was called *13,99 euros*: does the translation have to be retitled with each fluctuation in the exchange rate?). And these examples concern cultures that, all things considered, are fairly similar to each other. What of cultures that are radically dissimilar? Looking toward Middle Eastern and Asian literatures, the translator John Balcom wonders whether "even the most fluent translation" can be intelligible to Western readers "if the larger cultural context that generated the original work is not adequately understood."[19] In cases such as those, how does the translator convey the crucial background without adulterating the text or weighing it down unduly?

There is no one-size-fits-all answer: in the same work, one might encounter passages in which technical precision is paramount, others that underscore the music of the prose, and still others in which the comedy or pathos turns on a culture-specific reference. One sentence might require a scrupulous word-for-word tracing; another might benefit from a "stealth gloss," the quiet little insertion that whispers a bit of critical intel to the reader; still another might need to be broken down and rebuilt from scratch. The outcome often rests on the translator's abilities to recognize and confront each of these on its own terms—on having a sufficiently stocked tool kit and knowing how to use it.

Simply put, one's primary responsibility as a translator—to the reader, to the foreign author, to the text one is translating, to the culture that engendered it, and to oneself as a committed, caring professional—is to create a new literary text to the best of one's abilities and by whatever means appropriate. One that credibly represents the uniqueness of the source text, but also one that exudes as much life as the source text, and yields as much pleasure. Otherwise, why should anyone feel compelled to read it?

In this regard, I would suggest that one of the biggest pitfalls for translators is to become so concerned with theoretical or political strictures that they neglect those moments of pure, intuitive brilliance that constitute the joys of literature. Call this approach middle-of-the-road, or call it the refusal of a system, of an overarching theory that would force the translator toward a given strategy at the expense of another that might fit the particular bill more closely. Borges put it aptly: "When I translate Faulkner, I don't think about the problem of translating Faulkner."[20]

The bottom line is: every act is a political act, but a literary translation that "does wrong at home" will not remedy the world's inequities. All it will do is create one more unreadable volume to sit untouched on our shelves—assuming it gets that far—and help ruin yet another foreign author's chances of reaching a wider audience. It's as plain as that.

***

Any discussion of the ethics of translation necessarily includes the politics of publishing, and on this topic translators tend, for once, to be in dyspeptic consensus. While they may fight tooth and nail about methodology, with remarkably few exceptions they fall into lockstep on a set of basic complaints: that far too few translations are published in English (the frequently cited statistic is that, in the United States and United Kingdom combined, only about 2 to 3 percent of the books published each year are literary translations, though that figure has recently been revised up to about 5 percent—better, not great); that most editors are venal creatures who avoid translations because they're perceived as poor sellers; that when editors do publish translations, they tend to bowdlerize them and smooth out their difficulties to make them more marketable; that among published translations, a disproportionate number are from prominent Western languages, while the rest get short shrift; and so on.

As with any such charges, these contain their share of truth and exaggeration. It's true that the main Western European languages, French and Spanish in particular, do still account for the lion's share of English-language translations, though others have lately been coming up from behind; and that the Anglo-American publishing industry generally feels little need to gaze past its backyard: in contrast to our translation GDP of 5 percent, Western Europe and Latin America tend to translate at a rate of 20 to 40 percent. Taking the other tack, however, it is also true that a publisher's business is not only to bring good books to the world but also to *stay* in business, since an unsuccessful list does neither the publishing house nor its authors much good.

Regardless of the above, there are editors who regularly publish translations, who combat the indifference or skepticism of their colleagues and the media and labor to win these books the attention they deserve. And, picking up the mantle of illustrious predecessors like Alfred and Blanche Knopf, Helen and Kurt Wolff, and James Laughlin, there are a number of small independent presses, such as Archipelago, New Directions, Europa, Deep Vellum, Open Letter, Two Lines, Wakefield, and Dalkey Archive, who even in this day and age manage to survive largely, or even exclusively, on a diet of literary translations. There is also AmazonCrossing, the Web retailer's translation imprint, which is currently the most active publisher of literary translations in the United States.[21]

Nevertheless, the sad fact is that publishing translations is an uphill battle. The literary marketplace is as unpredictable as any other, and no one can really say why a Roberto Bolaño or Stieg Larsson, a Marguerite Duras or Umberto Eco (whose *Name of the Rose* reportedly made the rounds of New York publishers twice before Harcourt Brace picked it up), an Elena Ferrante or Karl Ove Knausgaard, breaks through and so many others don't; or why the long shot suddenly takes off while the surefire bestseller flops; or why a book that took the rest of the world by storm fizzles here. There are theories: the poor quality of foreign-language instruction in schools; the lack of a homogenous culture in the United States, making us more interested in the culture of our assimilation than of our (or others') heredity; the low profile of serious literature in general in this country and its lack of reach.[22] But these are at best partial explanations, not really an answer to a question that, ultimately, might not *have* an answer. What makes publishing both thrilling and challenging is that you never know in advance, and a good editor will launch each project into the world with the same level of hope, energy, and conviction, regardless of original language—even though for every translation that hits the bestseller list, there are many others that never recoup their costs, let alone make a profit. As the man said, publishing is a great way to end up with a small fortune, provided you start with a large one.

Let's consider the margins: if we take $15 as an average cover price for a translated novel in paperback, we can assume that about 50 percent of that will be scooped off the top in bookseller discounts (the average for most bookstores is 40 to 45 percent; Amazon, which accounts for many of these sales, charges as much as 55 percent), bringing the publisher's share per copy down to about $7.50. From this, remove a distribution fee that can go as high as 35 percent of net, or another $2.63, further reducing the share to $4.87. Assume a royalty, based on list price, of 8 percent to the foreign publisher ($1.20); that brings the publisher's earnings to $3.67 a copy. Now, assume up-front costs of about $5,000 in manufacturing and shipping based on a first printing of two thousand copies for a book of about two hundred pages (no illustrations), plus a translation fee of $6,000 (based on forty thousand words at the average rate of $150 per thousand), and the simple math says that you'll have to sell around 3,000 copies just to break even—more, in other words, than your entire first printing, and more, sadly, than most translations actually do sell. And this doesn't take into account overhead costs, warehousing, inventory depreciation, any promotional outlay, and other "invisible" expenses associated with publishing a book, even minimally.

Which is why strategies like foreignization ultimately come off as pure academic twaddle. For someone like Lawrence Venuti—and he's by no means alone—to plump for this approach as being "highly desirable today, a strategic intervention in the current state of world affairs"[23] while simultaneously bemoaning the translator's lot is simply perverse. Translations already suffer in this country from the assumption that their concerns, references, and form make them impenetrable to the American mind. They already run up against a prejudice that they are, by nature, financial sinkholes, only slightly tempered by the occasional success. Does anyone really believe that offering up even less approachable translations will help?

That's from the publisher's viewpoint. What about the translator's? Everyone knows the low rates most translators earn for their work, sometimes in stark contrast to the large advances the bestselling source author might command. It's true that

organizations such as PEN America have campaigned actively
to improve contractual terms for professional translators, and
that conditions today are, in the main, better than they once
were. But fees are still rather low—normally between 13 and
20 cents per word for a literary translator in the United States
(often rounded down if the book is long)—and royalties, if
offered at all, rarely exceed 1 or 2 percent of net proceeds (meaning that most translators never see any money beyond the initial advance). Even when there are subsidies from governments
wishing to promote the home culture abroad by making translations more affordable—the French have been particularly active
in this regard—very often the money only makes mildly cost-
effective what would have been ruinous before, and has little
impact on the translator's income. Tim Parks, one of translation's most outspoken curmudgeons (in a field that seems to
attract its fair share of them), recently advanced a controversial
proposal for doing away with royalties altogether and adopting
a payment scale based on the difficulty of the text, to be judged
by a combination of editor, translator, and expert in the field—a
nice idea in principle but a logistical nightmare and highly subjective to boot.[24]

Beyond questions of payment, but also related to publishing
economics, there is another difficulty inherent in the translator's
task: whereas an author might spend years grappling with the
mot juste, very often the translator, commissioned by an editor
on a tight production schedule, has only a matter of months
to wrestle with those same choices. The frequent combination
of limited income and limited time in which to earn it threatens to undermine the translator's personal investment in the
project (and therefore the end result), and calls uncomfortably
to mind Dryden's causative association between the dearth of

translators with "all the Talents" and their "small Encouragement"—an association that no doubt finds plenty of echo in
the dark basement of the translator's soul, where the little voices
whisper what society and literary history have always declared:
that he's a second-class citizen at best.

And what, finally, of the reviewers, whose job it is to inform,
evaluate, and champion? Among the most frequently cited
obstacles to winning a significant audience for translations is
the ever-dwindling stockpile of visible reviews that would ignite
interest in them—though perhaps websites such as GoodReads,
Bookslut, Omnivoracious, and Three Percent can help turn that
around.* Judging anecdotally, there does seem to be *slightly* more
review attention paid to translations at the moment than in
the recent past—a slightly good thing—though many reviewers
still display a certain reticence when dealing with foreign-born
works. We can see it in the noncommittal adverbs they tend
to favor when mentioning the translator's efforts, if mention is
made at all: *smoothly, fluidly, elegantly*, or that faintest of all faint
praises, *nicely*. Often the discussion begs the question of whether
the reviewer could or did read the original. Yes, there are some
who delve into the particulars of the translation, sometimes

---

* They have their work cut out for them, judging by this statement from
the former book-review editor of the *Atlantic Monthly* on how the magazine chooses titles for review: "We tend to focus on prose style in our assessment of fiction. It's obviously far more difficult to do so when review-
ing literature in translation, because both the reviewer and the reader of
the book encounter not the author's writing but the translator's rendering of it. Hence we run fewer pieces on translated works" (Benjamin
Schwarz, "Why We Review the Books We Do," *Atlantic Monthly*, January/
February 2004, accessed October 8, 2017, https://www.theatlantic.com/
magazine/archive/2004/01/new-noteworthy/302874/). The outrage that
greeted this statement appears to have had little effect on policy.

with acute perception, sometimes even with a degree of astig-
matic pedantry that threatens to kill any enjoyment the text
might offer. Most, on the other hand, simply take the English at
face value. In either case, what the reviewer is ultimately judging
is not the author's text but the translator's—a self-evident point
that too easily gets lost in discussions of "the author's" style, and
that translators, and the entire enterprise of translation, would
benefit from having made more explicit.

As both a translator and a publisher committed to translations, I'd be delighted to see more translations published, and
to be offered more books to translate. But I also have to wonder
whether many of the foreign works proposed for translation,
including ones that do find their way into print, are frankly
worth the effort. Granted, one man's Manchet is another man's
Cheate bread, but as a reader I'm probably as close to the target
demographic as any editor could wish, and even I find it hard
to get excited about many of the offerings—so just try foisting
them on your average Danielle Steele or Dan Brown fan (though
arguably *The Da Vinci Code* wouldn't exist without *The Name of
the Rose*, English version). Moreover, many of the translations I
hear about I discover by pure chance, even though I work in the
industry and presumably have better access to the information
than most. Which is why complaints about the crass mercan-
tilism of publishers, or about hegemonic imperatives proscrib-
ing certain languages from translation, often have a whiff of the
ivory tower about them. When it comes to suppressing foreign
voices, political machinations can't hold a candle to basic reader
indifference or lack of information.

To continue playing devil's advocate, I would add that many
of the pro-translation panels and other boosting efforts, however well-intentioned, exacerbate the problem by implying that
reading foreign literature is not so much a pleasure as a duty,

something good for you like medicine, and just as foul-tasting. There is an unpleasantly preachy tone to many arguments in favor of translation from "strange" cultures. "Little could be more relevant to the United States or to other nations in the contemporary world than the range of texts in need of translation," writes Sandra Bermann. "More and better translations of non-English texts could, for instance, clearly help the Anglo-American reader to engage literary worlds and historical cultures that are not her own." Yes, but who said the reader wants to engage? And what makes these texts that are purportedly "in need of translation" more relevant to even a reasonably cultured American than professional, personal, and financial concerns, or than the plethora of other cultural events vying for her attention? Similarly, Edith Grossman states flat out that "publishing houses in the United States and the United Kingdom have an ethical and cultural responsibility to foster literature in translation." A responsibility to whom? Too often such admonitions fall on closed ears because of their distinct undertone of street-corner proselytizing, anathema even to sympathetic listeners, and because they fail to address the deeply ingrained streak of insularity in the American makeup. Because of this insularity, it is all too easy for the public at large, and the critical and publishing establishment in its wake, to dismiss non-English books, even beautifully translated ones, as "too foreign," "too cold," "too hot," "too other," or to ignore them altogether. Our nation was founded on an ideal of "self-reliance." We are, as Andre Dubus III wrote, "isolated between two oceans and have friendly neighbors to the north and south and can afford the luxury of being provincial"—the luxury of believing that America, as the bombastic, blinkered slogan has it, "comes first." Simply denying or decrying this fact won't make it go away.[25] And before we condemn too shrilly the intellectual lethargy of John Q. Reading-Public, we translators and culturati would do well to heal ourselves. Some years ago, at an American Literary Translators Association colloquium, I asked how many in the audience had purchased a translated book in the past twelve months; a very small number of hands (2 to 3 percent, perhaps?) shot up.

I say all this not because I don't believe in the power of translation—quite the opposite—but because I believe literary translation serves a purpose somewhat adjacent to the roles of cultural reeducation or global unity that we tend to assign to it. Translation is like any art: in the best of cases, it helps shed light on ourselves, on those hidden corners of ourselves that we barely knew existed, and whose discovery has enriched us. It exposes us to minds and voices able to awaken in us a particular sense of delight, an irreplaceable thrill of discovery that is available nowhere else. The ability of these minds and voices to do this is unique, not because they come from a foreign land—or at least, not solely because of it—but because they are sui generis, as exceptional in their own culture as they appear in ours. If literary translation is valuable in today's world, it is because such minds and voices are exceedingly rare, and we cannot afford to be ignorant of a single one of them. And if publishers indeed ought to publish more translations, it is not because they are "good for us," in that annoying, finger-wagging sense, but because such voices, in whatever language they have originally expressed themselves, are the reason that humans have hungered after stories since consciousness began.

That, at least, is the ideal. The reality is that publishing choices are often dictated not so much by the work's intrinsic qualities, or by recommendations from translators or professors of foreign literatures, or even by its commercial prospects, though all of those factor into them—no, what most often drives the choice is happenstance, availability: the fact that a certain rights manager at the Frankfurt Book Fair caught a certain editor's attention with an author's work, or that some nations actively promote their literatures abroad while others don't, or that far more book editors in this country can read French or Spanish than, say, Estonian or Urdu. In other words, most editors, even well-disposed, are very often flying blind.

In order to help remedy this situation, to combat that insularity mentioned above, we need to start much further back than a publisher's office. We need to start in homes and in schools, by nurturing in our children, and in ourselves, the attitude that foreign languages, foreign literatures, foreign viewpoints, matter. That they are not something to be kept to the other side of some mythical wall but welcomed into our homes and integrated into our daily lives. Because if this attitude does not become part of our thinking patterns and our buying habits, then it is only natural that fewer and fewer foreign books will be offered for sale, with the result that our exposure to these viewpoints will continue to diminish. And our cultural perspectives—our perspectives as human beings in the world—might well atrophy beyond repair.

5   The Silences Between

The American anthropologist Laura Bohannan once tried to paraphrase *Hamlet* for a tribe of West African bush people. Convinced that "human nature is pretty much the same the whole world over," Bohannan chose *Hamlet* as a reliable universal archetype. It sounds good on paper, but at practically every sentence, she found her listeners raising objections and interpolations wholly outside her frame of reference:

> "Polonius [Bohannan narrates] insisted that Hamlet was mad because he had been forbidden to see Ophelia, whom he loved."
>
> "Why," inquired a bewildered voice, "should anyone bewitch Hamlet on that account?"
>
> "Bewitch him?"
>
> "Yes, only witchcraft can make anyone mad." ...
>
> "Laertes [she later resumes] came back for his father's funeral. The great chief told him Hamlet had killed Polonius. Laertes swore to kill Hamlet because of this, and because his sister Ophelia, hearing her father had been killed by the man she loved, went mad and drowned in the river."
>
> "Have you already forgotten what we told you?" The old man was reproachful. "One cannot take vengeance on a madman; Hamlet killed Polonius in his madness. As for the girl, she not only went mad, she was drowned. Only witches can make people drown. Water itself can't hurt anything. It is merely something one drinks and

bathes in. ... [Laertes therefore] killed his sister by witchcraft, drowning her so he could secretly sell her body to the witches."

Finally, losing patience with Bohannan's "errors," the tribal
elder takes over the narration altogether, concluding, "Sometime you must tell us some more stories of your country. We,
who are elders, will instruct you in their true meaning, so that
when you return to your own land your elders will see that you
have not been sitting in the bush, but among those who know
things and who have taught you wisdom."[1]

As Bohannan discovered the hard way, even supposedly universal truths get filtered through highly local perspectives, and
words resonate differently from one country, one collective, one
people, to the next. "A language," as Noam Chomsky observed,
"is not just words. It's a culture, a tradition, a unification of a
community, a whole history that creates what a community
is." "Dog," in whichever idiom, signifies *Canis familiaris*, but
associatively the dog does not mean the same thing to someone who is English, French, or Chinese. Gregory Rabassa has
remarked that if you ask a New Yorker what kind of bug Gregor
Samsa metamorphosed into, "the inevitable answer will be a
giant cockroach, the insect of record in his city," even though
Kafka's term, *Ungeziefer*, means simply "vermin." Similarly, the
Russian translator Richard Lourie cautioned that the term *com-
munal apartment* in English "conjures up an image of a Berkeley,
California kitchen, where hippies with headbands are cooking
brown rice, whereas the Russian term [*kommunalka*] evokes a
series of vast brown rooms with a family living in each, sharing
a small kitchen where the atmosphere is dense with everything
that cannot be said."[2]

At issue here is translation not so much between languages as
between cultures, the most recalcitrant text of all, and the most

difficult to anticipate. Even a highly representative translation faces the challenge that different readerships read differently. To put it another way: even though readers are not a homogenous block, even within the source culture, at least they share a relatively similar set of associations and secondary meanings, which the author can play upon or take for granted in writing the book. Transpose that set of associations into a culture with its own, dissimilar set of givens, and who knows what will happen? As the writer and translator Tim Parks notes, "However much the writer may prize his individual identity, his book is not the same book in another context."[3]

It's true that, to some degree, at least, a great work transcends these disparities. To paraphrase an old ad for Levy's rye bread, you don't have to be Jewish—or Czech—to love Kafka. But can you love him in the same way? Beyond any linguistic acrobatics the work requires or references demanding explication, there are ambient assumptions that refuse to be ferried across. And just as the book changes with the context, so too does the translation strategy.

For instance, a text in French tends to run longer than the same text in English, usually by 10 to 20 percent. (On that score, I once had the humbling experience of finding that my translation of a short story by Jean Echenoz, who writes remarkably economical prose, was actually longer than the French original. Much paring ensued.) This is true even on the level of sentences, which according to the rules of good French usage can be longer than English normally allows. What this means is that, in general, a lengthy sentence in French will pass as business as usual to a French reader, but will be perceived as excessively wordy to an English one. The translator wishing to maintain a representative effect might well need to repunctuate, sometimes to break the sentence in two or three. This is not a universally accepted principle, and many accomplished translators would call this a blatant example of abusive domestication. It's also not a universally applicable principle: Proust's marathon utterances, for instance, are lengthy even by French standards and are characteristic of his style; in that case, one needs at least to suggest the unusual extent of his phrasing, without at the same time getting so entangled in the subclauses as to produce gobbledygook. (Much as a few writers in English, such as James Baldwin, have handled impossibly long sentences with grace.) In general, though, I would argue that judicious restructuring brings you closer to the author's desired effect than a close parallel. As an example, Lawrence Venuti's comparison of two versions of a forty-word passage by Françoise Sagan, one by himself (forty-two words), one in the published translation by Irene Ash (twenty-nine words), shows, perhaps inadvertently, how much closer Ash comes to Sagan's tone and punch, while Venuti's ostensibly more accurate calque just makes it sound dull.[4]

Cultural adaptations can take many forms, often passing by unnoticed, or noticed only when they fail. There's a scene in Quentin Tarantino's film *Inglourious Basterds* in which an American soldier in a *Bierhalle*, who until then has managed to pass as German, orders three beers, with the corresponding finger gesture. Unfortunately, as an alert intelligence officer observes, he does it with the standard American configuration—thumb and pinky looped, index through ring extended—rather than the European: thumb through middle extended, last two folded down. By not translating the gesture into the target norm, he gives himself away and unleashes a bloodbath.

The export of popular films is a frequent arena of cultural adaptation, the main intent being, as with Eugene Nida's Bibles, not so much to pass as native as to draw in the crowd. The title of Sofia Coppola's *Lost in Translation*, appropriately enough, underwent any number of international transformations, from the fairly literal ("Unfaithful translation" in Canadian French, "Between words" in German) to more creative options, such as "Lost in Tokyo" in Latin American Spanish and "Meetings and missed meetings" in Brazilian Portuguese (but "Love in a strange place" in European Portuguese). Not even as seemingly straightforward a title as *Annie Hall* survived the voyage, becoming "Two strange lovers" in Latin America and the harsh but not inaccurate "Urban neurotic" in Germany—though whether that refers to Diane Keaton's character or Woody Allen's is unclear.[5]

Advertising is a still more fertile ground for adaptations and pitfalls. Everyone has seen foreign food products with names that wouldn't play in Peoria, including Urinal tea and Pee Cola, Child Shredded Meat, Barfy frozen patties, Only Puke snack chips, Plopp and Fart candy bars ... fill in your own examples. And it's not only about names. A bilingual ad for Air Canada, featuring a husband and wife flying to New York, shows how the narrative is retweaked to suit alternate sets of assumptions: in the English version, Mr. Jackson is "on his way to close an important deal," while his wife is smiling because "Mr. Jackson didn't leave her behind this trip"; in the French, M. Gauthier is simply traveling "on business," while Madame is "happy for this distraction from the daily routine, happy to be with him."[6] The information is the same, but the message has been altered to appeal to the more "businesslike" Anglo and "romantic" Franco sensibilities. Anyone reading the bilingual in-flight magazines of certain airlines or international trains will notice a similar phenomenon. And the Vatican, never one to miss a trick, offers

Latin instructions at its automatic cash machine for the resolutely nonsecular (the ancient Romans apparently called their
ATM cards *scidulae*).

As is well known to any translator, one of the hardest, most
culture-bound registers to translate is slang. The topic has been
discussed at length and there are as many solutions—or nonso-
lutions—as there are instances to solve. Richard Howard, speaking of French "low life" texts like the *roman noir* (but a similar
claim could be made for any number of languages), points out
that "the French have developed a middle language somewhere
between the smell of the sewer and the smell of the lamp,"
whereas the closest corresponding English slang tends toward
"either the very coarse or the very clinical." In other words, even
a private dick in an American noir will not swear like his *flic*
counterpart (leaving aside the fact that most of the French Série
Noire crime novels supposedly translated "from the American"
were actually written by French writers, using American-sound-
ing pseudonyms to make the books more marketable).[7]

The opportunities for misunderstanding are rife even within
the same language, as demonstrated by the recent estrangement
of Quebecois and French into two increasingly distinct idioms.
As the French-Canadian sociologist Marcel Rioux put it, "Even
when the words are the same, they express another reality,
another experience."[8] For Quebecers, the impulse is unabashedly nationalistic, a will to assert an identity of their own, not
only against the English-speaking rest of the country but also
vis-à-vis the imported culture of France, which many feel no longer reflects their particular concerns. The result, in yet another
instance of two nations divided by a common language, is that
texts, especially plays, are being retranslated directly into *joual* to
make them more accessible to Quebec audiences, slowly pushing

the French of France toward incomprehensibility. And sometimes the miscommunication goes beyond speech altogether.
The story is told of an American professor in Japan who believed
from his colleagues' comments that they had just settled a cam-
pus strike, only to realize later that the opposite was true. "You
understood all the words correctly," he was told, "but you did
not understand the silences between them."[9]

***

How does one bridge those silences? There is of course no set
formula, but there are issues and techniques with which a translator frequently grapples in the quest for a convincing representation that will speak across cultural gaps. These are: style and
voice, transformation and adaptation, and reading and interpretation. While these might seem mere matters of technique, they
are in fact part and parcel of the aesthetic package that a translator labors to create, for an author's style and its reception by the
source audience are as culturally determined as is the translator's
interpretation of it.

The matter of style is among the thorniest problems in the
translator's rucksack of woes. How does one re-create something
as personal and idiosyncratic as the "crucial and elusive quality of voice" and make it resonate in a foreign context? How
does one pinpoint it? Where does one locate what David Bellos calls "the Dickensianity of any text by Dickens"? Is it "in
the words, the sentences, the paragraphs, the digressions, the
anecdotes, the construction of character, or the plot"?[10] Authors
who are liable to become part of the world literary canon, who
are deemed worthy of translation, often have a distinctive way
of expressing themselves, one that helps define their work and
attract readers to it, and without which they would not be who
they are. Despite their shared preoccupation with memory,

Proust does not sound like Modiano; nor does Hemingway sound like Fitzgerald, despite their Lost Generational affiliation.

"Every question of style can also become a question of translation," writes the novelist Adam Thirlwell. "Another description of an accurate translation, I think, can be a voluntary pastiche, a reproduction of the style." On this score, Doris Lessing no doubt spoke for many writers when she lamented, "I work so hard on style, and then find out that in translation a sentence has become flat and monotonous."[11] As an author who has been translated myself, I've had similar experiences, finding the particular humor or resonance that I had labored to put into a sentence turned into cardboard. But I also once noticed an interesting phenomenon: in a translation into French, a language I know well, the style had been erased, whereas with the same text in German, which I could read only with the original at hand, I was nevertheless able to verify that the style had come through more or less intact. There is something about style, as a quality, that seems to transcend linguistic comprehension.

Marcel Proust, for his part, defined style less in terms of words and more as "the transformation that the author's thought imposes on reality,"[12] in other words as the shape the author's particular understanding gives to his expression. And that, with the right empathy, is something that *can* be translated. Proust himself provides an instructive case study. His first and most renowned translator, C. K. Scott Moncrieff, began his work during Proust's lifetime, inspired by a feeling of compatibility. Both men had lived through World War I; they shared a passion for art, literature, and genealogy, all of which are central to *À la recherche du temps perdu*. As a man of letters born into privilege, openly gay in bohemian circles but closeted vis-à-vis his rigid family, a Scotsman in England, and a product of his Edwardian times, Scott Moncrieff enjoyed an almost instinctive kinship with Proust—also born into privilege, also leading a double life because of his sexuality, a Jew in Dreyfus-era Paris, writing in the same Edwardian years in which Scott Moncrieff came of age— that allowed the translator to enter into the skin of the book. So much so, apparently, that he could read a passage in the original, jot the translation into his notebook, and hold a conversation all at the same time.

Before his premature death, Scott Moncrieff managed to translate six of Proust's seven volumes, the first published in 1922. Joseph Conrad praised his translation as having a quality of "revelation" that the original lacked, F. Scott Fitzgerald called it "a masterpiece in itself," and even Proust recognized its "fine talent" (with some inevitable quibbles). It's true that Scott Moncrieff's version contains lapses and errors, due both to his imperfect French and, no doubt, to his conversational multitasking: it remains in print today partly on its own merits, and partly because subsequent rounds of revisions, by Terence Kilmartin, D. J. Enright, and William C. Carter, have corrected its more egregious gaffes. Scott Moncrieff's English can also sound a bit fussy to twenty-first-century ears. But as a reviewer of the recent Penguin retranslation (by various hands) wrote in 2002, "Scott Moncrieff, for all his occasional carelessness and prissiness, was probably temperamentally better suited than many later translators to making sense of [Proust's] style. ... For the Penguin translators, one feels, this version of Proust is a job well done; for Scott Moncrieff, it was a labor of love." Lydia Davis, one of the Penguin translators, offered a different, but not *wholly* different, view when she noted that Scott Moncrieff's version "was written in an Edwardian English more dated than Proust's own prose, and it departed consistently from the French original. Yet it had such conviction, on its own terms, and was so well written, if you liked a certain florid style, that it prevailed without competition for eighty years."[13] If, as D. H. Lawrence posited, the style "is natural to the author," a visceral thing, then sometimes it takes a certain amount of visceral connection—perhaps aided by shared experiences, milieu, or times—to bring that style across.

In attempting to bring that style across, some translators have tried to turn authors from other ages into de facto contemporaries. John Dryden, like many before and since, "endeavoured to make Virgil speak such English as he would himself have spoken, if he had been born in England, and in this present age." At first glance, this seems reasonable enough: rendering Virgil into "ancient" English would ring false (for one thing, there was no English in Virgil's time), just as it would be ludicrous for a translator today to translate Montaigne into the language of his contemporary Shakespeare. That said, a translation overly marked by its own time and place threatens to become dated all the more quickly: Dryden's Virgil spoke to his seventeenth-century audience, but despite some lasting beauties, it has long shown its age. As centuries pass and literary fashions evolve, so too do readers' expectations. Pope's Homer has since been replaced by Lattimore's, Fitzgerald's, and Fagles's, just as theirs will be eventually be replaced by others. Walter Benjamin foresaw this when he wrote, "While a poet's words endure in his own language, even the greatest translation is destined to become part of the growth of its own language and eventually to be absorbed by its renewal."[14]

Moreover, while contemporaneity between author and translator can cultivate intuitive sympathy, there are also distinct advantages to hindsight. The more resources accrue over time, from the latest research to precursors' hits and misses, the better it can be for future translators. Sometimes the passage of years is necessary to reveal a text to another culture. One could argue that Rimbaud's modernity didn't fully emerge until the counter-culture movement of the 1960s lent credence to his attitudes, allowing recent translations to capture his tone more convincingly than did, for instance, Louise Varèse's in the 1940s. Similarly, when retranslating Flaubert's *Bouvard and Pécuchet*, I discovered the twentieth-century quality of its prose and perspective, which I found in none of the previous English versions. Looking at the text from a world in which Samuel Beckett, Jim Jarmusch, and Jerry Seinfeld are fixtures of the landscape, it seemed to me that Flaubert's comic morality play, with its deadpan affect and cynical take on human motivations, was speaking in a thoroughly modern, Anglo-friendly idiom. The reductio ad absurdam example is Borges's "Pierre Menard, Author of Don Quixote," in which the language of the *Quixote*, as written by Cervantes, is merely "the ordinary Spanish of his time," but when re-created verbatim by the twentieth-century poet Menard becomes "almost infinitely richer."[15]

Two recent translations of Kafka's novel *Amerika*, by Michael Hofmann and Mark Harman, based on the restored German manuscript, seek to update our understanding of Kafka by going back to the basics. Both translations offer Anglophone readers the uncompleted novel just as Kafka left it, before Max Brod did his posthumous tailoring, which was preserved by the first English translators, Willa and Edwin Muir. Both of these new versions also return to Kafka's working title, *Der Verschollene* (rendered as *The Man Who Disappeared* by Hofmann and *The Missing Person* by Harman) and reinstate several unfinished passages. Finally, both seek to re-create the jaggedness of Kafka's prose, his willed contrast between naturalness and theatricality—an effect particularly pronounced in *Amerika*, which concerns the Felliniesque misadventures in the New World of one Karl Rossmann. There is a stagy stiffness to the narrative and the characters' speech that leaves the translator caught between the desire to retain and the danger of appearing inept. Following Brod's lead, the Muirs laundered much of this stiffness out, along with Kafka's unkempt syntax and factual slips (such as his mention of a bridge linking Manhattan not to Brooklyn but to Boston). Indeed, they later wrote of wanting "to write an English prose as natural in the English way as [Kafka's] was in his own way"[16]—though according to these new translations, Kafka's prose was not very natural at all. The Muirs had their reasons, of course: publishing their translation only fourteen years after Kafka's death, they were seeking to introduce an author barely known to the English-speaking world, just as Brod had done for German readers a mere decade before. Hofmann and Harman, on the other hand, have the luxury of translating a writer who has since become a household name, and this gives them the freedom to render *Amerika* with all its imperfections gloriously intact. In a word, their Kafka no longer has anything to prove.

Neither, at this point, does Camus. Returning for a moment to *The Stranger*'s iconic opening (see chapter 3): Ryan Bloom, in the *New Yorker*, takes issue with Stuart Gilbert's well-known version, *Mother died today*, arguing that *Mother* is too uncaring, and that Gilbert's reordering of Camus's sentence (literally, "Today, Mother died") obscures its " 'mystical' deeper meaning," which requires placing the mother between the immediacy of "today" and the eternity of death. Bloom's solution is to keep Camus's order and retain the French *Maman* (as in Matthew Ward's retranslation): *Today, Maman died.*[17] I can't agree. The laconic weariness of Meursault, announced as of that first utterance, requires the "smoother, more natural" syntax that Bloom rejects. And while I take his point that *Mother* sounds rather impersonal, I also believe that thrusting a foreign word at the reader right from the start, even one as decipherable as *Maman*, puts up a roadblock that Camus's French audience never faced. This one word aside, I believe the exact sequence counts for less in this case than the matter-of-fact, nondescript way in which Meursault expresses a major life trauma, avoiding anything that would attract undue attention or sympathy. A more recent translation, by Sandra Smith, comes closer to a solution by adding a personal touch: *My mother died today.**

Time is the enemy of all perishable products and books are no exception. As evidenced by a number of current retranslations of classic works—Proust and Camus are two examples; the much ballyhooed reworkings of nineteenth-century Russians by cotranslators Richard Pevear and Larissa Volokhonsky are another—the trend is toward greater precision, correction of past mistakes, and stricter adherence to the original vocabulary and syntax. There is no question that translations need periodic updating and correction—I've indulged in a few retranslations myself—but, to sound a note of caution amid the roar of applause, this can be a Pyrrhic victory. The attempt to improve on a forerunner's shortcomings sometimes ends up lessening the pleasure of the text, and the gains don't always compensate for the losses. There is something to be said for certain older translations, however flawed, that have grafted themselves onto our experience of a given work through circumstance or familiarity, that have made their way into our literary culture, and that refuse to be shouldered aside even by younger, better-endowed contenders.

E. T. A. Hoffmann's "The Sandman," the tale of the student Nathanael's fatal obsession with an automaton and its creator,

---

* Just as deceptively simple, and just as tricky, is the book's title: the French word *étranger* refers equally to an unknown person and a foreigner, which British editions have nicely captured by calling the novel *The Outsider*. But it is the more homophonic, less semantically accurate *The Stranger* that has prevailed, at least in the United States.

has spawned several English translations, but none so affecting in my view as a slightly ungainly version by Michael Bullock, published in 1963. Though dotted with awkward phrasings ("I say, Mama, who is this naughty Sandman who always drives us away from Papa?"), Bullock's "Sandman" somehow brings home the horror and degradation of Nathanael's infatuation with the lifeless Olympia, his dealings with the baneful Coppelius, and his descent into madness in a way that no other translation I've seen has managed. Similarly, despite its technically superior successors, I admit to a lingering fondness for the 1937 Muir translation of Kafka's *The Trial*: "Someone must have traduced Joseph K., for without having done anything wrong he was arrested one fine morning." There are, no doubt, more natural and contemporary ways to express this: recent translations have replaced the earlier verb with more natural-sounding synonyms such as *slandered* or *spread lies about*. But what could spell betrayal and defamation, in all their moral and legalistic obscenity, better than fusty old *traduced*? It just sounds more Kafkaesque. Such filaments, often unheeded by the reader, perhaps also by the translator, weave the matrix in which moments of magic flourish, lingering in the mind years after one encounters them, even after the rest of the work has darkened into oblivion.

Does this sound like the proverbial cake-and-eat-it-too argument? No doubt. But then, what's wrong with having multiple translations at our disposal? Who said we *have* to choose among available versions? Why not savor them all, the scrupulous as well as the fanciful, in an endlessly renewable banquet?

Where things begin to get truly sticky is when an author's style willfully deforms its own language. It's a fact that translation pushes language a bit more toward standardized usage, even when a translator tries to respect the original's stylistic unorthodoxies. What happens when these unorthodoxies are integral to the work? Is Céline's "J'espère qu'à l'heure actuelle il est bien crevé (et pas d'une mort pépère)" fully rendered by Ralph Manheim's "I hope they've killed him off by now (and not pleasantly)"?[18] Not really. But the bitterness and cynicism of Céline's voice is there for all to see, if not the particular flair with which Céline spits it out.

The difficulties are highlighted in another recent retranslation, of Günter Grass's *The Tin Drum* by Breon Mitchell. Discussing (again) Ralph Manheim's much-read version in his afterword, Mitchell contrasts his predecessor's "smooth and readable" English to one that "clings closer to the author":

> He was also the Formella brothers' boss and was glad to make our acquaintance, just as we were glad to make his. (Manheim)

> He was also the Formella brothers' boss, and was pleased, as we were pleased, to meet us, to meet him. (Mitchell)

Mitchell's point is that in this passage, Grass has caught "his German reader's attention by allowing the introductions to cross each other, as they often do in real life, rearranging and interlocking the grammatical structure of the sentence," and that Mitchell has retained the effect in English. This is no doubt true, the problem being that Grass's interlocked German (especially if we read the translation without the benefit of Mitchell's gloss, on which in fact it should not be dependent) here comes out merely as twisted English.

Similarly, Mitchell describes how Grass's string of neologisms—"Daumendrehen, Strirnrunzeln, Köpfchensenken, Händeschütteln, Kindermachen, Falschgeldprägen, Lichtausknipsen, Zähneputzen, Totschießen und Trockenlegen"—can best be conveyed by "stretching the [English] language a little: 'thumb-twiddling, brow-wrinkling, head-nodding, hand-shaking, baby-making, coin-faking, light-dousing, tooth-brushing, man-killing and diaper-changing.' "[19] It's an inventive solution, and the "shaking ... making ... faking" series provides a nice comic touch. But such wordamalgamations pass much more naturally in German, while in English they have an effect not unlike the verb at the end of the sentence putting. One could also argue that whereas writing happens on the level of words (though this is far from certain), translation happens on the level of sentences, or of paragraphs. The point is that, even while being "playful and inventive" in his native tongue, Grass is creating an effect of surprise and delight in his reader. Trying to mirror it too closely in another language that plays by other rules creates nothing more than irritation.

Perhaps a truly representative version of an idiosyncratic style requires the liberties that can be taken only by the author himself, as when Joyce rewrote "Anna Livia Plurabelle" in French and Italian, using his profound knowledge of those target languages to re-create the plurilingualism of his English in a stylistically meaningful way. Umberto Eco even affirmed that "to understand *Finnegans Wake*, it would be a good idea to start with [Joyce's] Italian translation of it." The critic Michael Wood notes how Nabokov's French-language story "Mademoiselle O.," though treated to a "perfectly competent translation" by Adam Thirlwell, "becomes memorable ... only when Nabokov himself rewrites it" for *Speak, Memory*.[20] It's a commonplace that one has a uniquely intimate relation with one's own text. This extends as well to the translation of that text, which can yield unexpected discoveries. Once, when I undertook to translate some poems of mine into French, the exercise not only highlighted my limitations in that familiar but foreign tongue, the subtleties and resources that still eluded me, but also brought out layers of meaning in the English originals that I hadn't realized were there.

Moreover, the author rewriting himself in another language is not the same author who composed the original text: the process and the context are different, as is the linguistic medium, as is the readership. Rabindranath Tagore recognized this, in consciously adapting his own English translations of his Bengali poems to suit Western expectations. Kundera recognized it too, even while railing against translators who dared make stylistic alterations: the "improved" translation of his novel *The Joke*, a mix of his own and previous versions, makes, by Lawrence Venuti's count, more than fifty alterations and deletions from the Czech. Comments Venuti: "When the author is the translator, apparently, he is not above the domestication that he attacked in the previous English versions."[21]

In the final account, as the translator Susan Bernofsky put it, "All translation is transformation. It just isn't possible for a text to work in its new language and context in exactly the same way it worked in the original." If one is to respect the text one is translating, if one wishes to honor it with whatever measure of "fidelity" one can possibly offer, then some degree of change is inevitable. The devilish details will govern just how much change, and of what nature, and how successful one is, but somewhere along the line some adaptation will intervene. You can translate Catullus in classic verse; or in hipster jive, as did Frank O. Copley in the Fifties: "just do that like I tell you ol' pal ol' pal / you'll get a swell dinner … I CAN'T GIVE YOU ANYTHING BUT LOVE, BABY"; or, as did Celia and Louis Zukofsky, in homophonic interpretation, so that "Nulli se dicit mulier mea nubere malle" ("My woman says there is no one she would rather marry") becomes "Newly say dickered my love air my own would marry me all." *A Night of Serious Drinking*, the English title of René Daumal's novel *La grande beuverie* (literally, "The big carouse"), is an adaptation in that it forgoes the brevity and syntactical form of the original, but nonetheless perfectly conveys Daumal's tone, and makes for a great title to boot. Whether or not any given instance works is up to the reader to judge. The point is to allow Catullus and Daumal to speak as best they can across nebulous cultural boundaries, and not lie mute and moribund on the page.[22]

Like any form of reading, translation is an act of interpretation, based on individual experience and cultural conditioning as much as on any supposedly universal givens. We need only compare variant translations of a text to see how readings can differ, and how manifold are the resources that translators can bring to the expression of those readings. Gregory Rabassa points out that it is "a common notion to say that if a work has 10,000 readers it becomes 10,000 different books. … [The translator's] reading, then, becomes the one reading that is going to spawn 10,000 varieties of the book" in the target language. The exponentially expanding degrees of ambiguity involved, from the many possible understandings of the source text by source-language readers to the multiple interpretations by different translators to the unpredictable receptions of those translations, and so on, make it easy to see why the scholar Matthew Reynolds characterizes literary translation as a series of "loose approximations,"[23] in which any hope of a definitive version—much like any hope of a definitive understanding between cultures—is chimerical. And so much the better.

6 Sympathy for the Traitor

Every translator's origin story seems to involve a measure of serendipity, and mine is no exception. Forty-odd years ago, a set of improbable circumstances found me sitting across a café table from the French novelist Maurice Roche. I was seventeen at the time, faking my way through university courses in Paris. Roche was around fifty, a well-known figure associated with the fashionable Tel Quel group, which included some of the day's most hotly discussed writers. His latest novel, *CodeX*, had been on the syllabus of one of my courses. Roche himself had just addressed the class, and now here I was face-to-face with him, a Real Live Author.

For those too young to remember, *Tel Quel* was a journal that more or less dominated French intellectual life in the Sixties and Seventies. Its editors included Philippe Sollers, Julia Kristeva, Jacques Derrida, and especially Roland Barthes, who at the time was France's preeminent public thinker. The books published under the journal's eponymous imprint—mainly theory or fiction, and often a mix of the two—were known to be difficult, written in deliberately challenging language. They even looked intimidating, uniformly issued in stark white covers with a sober brown border. Buying one of them felt like committing an obscure revolutionary act.

Reading *CodeX* fully justified my sense of exhilaration and trepidation. Its concatenation of word games, cultural arcana, pictograms, references to everything from Rabelais to Joyce to recent headlines, foreign words, portmanteau words, invented words, and typographical hijinks pushed the limits of reader tolerance. Some sentences had words shifted to a separate line above, causing them to bifurcate (as in the example below). An entire section of the novel was based on Mozart's *Requiem*, with the Latin text transposed into French words that sounded the same but created their own, separate, comic narrative. I was no babe in the avant-garde woods, but I hadn't a clue what to make of this. And as I dutifully struggled my way through Roche's bewildering parade of puns, assonances, and triple and quadruple entendres, I could only shake my head in wonder at how utterly untranslatable it all seemed. Yet here I was, sitting with the author at a café. The mutual friend who'd brought us there had gone to make a phone call, and I could think of no better icebreaker than, "Gee, Mr. Roche, it sure would be interesting to translate your novel into English!" Instead of the expected silence or polite brush-off, my blurted offer was met with bright-eyed enthusiasm, and over the next two years I translated both *CodeX* (poorly) and (with a bit more success) Roche's earlier novel, *Compact*.

What were some of the challenges? Here's a sample from *CodeX*:

Don Juan $\overset{\text{prenant son}}{\text{au petit}}$ pied, troud*balisant* en qué-quête d'absolu
—et levant le coude à la santé de veuve poignante:

(les queues en l'air sont pour la main droite)

This I gamely attempted to render as follows:

Don Juan steady on his feet, *groping* in cock-quest of the absolute
with cold
—and bending an elbow to the health of Miss *Palm*er:

(upright stems are played with the right hand)

If I wanted to go easy on myself, I'd say that enough of the meaning and wordplay come through to keep this from being a complete flop. Still, dissatisfactions fester. *Steady on his feet* is not the same as *prenant son pied*—which means both "to enjoy greatly" and "to come," in the orgasmic sense—but I needed to preserve the shared final word. (Alternately, I could have gone with something like *getting his kicks*, assuming I could find an appropriate second phrase to end on *kicks*.) *Troudbalisant*, a portmanteau combining the slang for "asshole" (*trou de balle*) with the verb for "marking out," gives a sense of zoning in on an explicit anatomical area that *groping* only suggests, and gone is the verbal interpenetration. *Veuve poignante* ("poignant widow") is a play on *veuve poignet* (literally, "Widow Wrist," slang for masturbation); my rendering "Miss *Palm*er," though it gets the hand in, relies clumsily on italics for the overtone of self-abuse. You get the picture.

Roche's *Compact* posed a different set of challenges. The novel consists of seven distinct narratives, each assigned a specific typeface (boldface, italics, small caps, etc.) that corresponds to a specific person (I, you, he, one, it) and a specific tense (past, present, future, conditional). These have then been hacked up and spliced together like bits of audiotape to form a new, composite narrative, even as each retains its own integrity and continuity.

Which means that *Compact* can be read either straight through, following the interweaving strands as they occur, or one narrative at a time. I sometimes felt that I was dealing with a Tristan Tzara poem made out of random newspaper clippings, or one of the Beats' cutups, except that I had to make each fragment match a corresponding one later in the text, while still trying to convey Roche's carefully orchestrated rhythm and syntax.

Because of how *Compact* is constructed, but also because of Roche's love of wordplay and verbal effects, at times I had to adapt more than translate. To take one small example, the novel's main protagonist is a blind man who lives in a Paris garret and is prey to unwelcome visitors, including a young American woman whose speech is a mix of Anglicisms and the kind of heavily Yankified French that one hears in cafés throughout the Latin Quarter. Seeing no direct way to retain this effect, I turned the *Américaine* (pronounced à la Jean Seberg) into a *Frrrensh girl*, her comic intonation and foreign mannerisms intact. No doubt another translator would have arrived at a different way of handling it. As for me, it's the way that made the most sense at the time, based on my reading not only of the novel but also of Roche as a writer, of his sensibility, of the note he was trying to sound (and as it turned out, he liked it).

Several decades and a few dozen books later, I translated Linda Lê's *The Three Fates*, a "translation" of *King Lear* into a novel about three Vietnamese women living in contemporary France. Lê is herself a Vietnamese-born novelist who writes in French. Like many other xenophonic authors—Beckett, Nabokov, Conrad, Ionesco, and (more recently) Jhumpa Lahiri come to mind—she approaches her new tongue as one might a beloved but curious object, twisting and turning it in all directions, admiring its contours but nonetheless wanting to see what happens when it gets wrenched out of shape. The artist and writer Leonora Carrington, who composed many of her stories in rudimentary French or Spanish, considered that linguistic unfamiliarity crucial: "I was not hindered by a preconceived idea of the words, and I but half understood their modern meaning. This made it possible for me to invest the most ordinary phrases with a hermetic significance."[1]

In Lê's case, I get the sense that it's the *plasticity* of the idiom that fascinates her, even more than its meanings. In seeking to represent the sinuous, assonant, etymologically savvy, and very frayed nature of her language, I had to do the same things to my own, which at times led me to create as much as re-create, for Lê's prose demands active participation. In some passages, for example, she takes a common idiom—such as *feuille de choux*, referring to a cheap tabloid or "gutter rag"—and runs with it, stretching it out through pages of extended metaphor. For this, I tried to work the literal definition of that expression, *cabbage leaf*, as naturally as possible into my translation, so that it could then be *planted*, *watered*, and *fertilized* as needed. To give another example, a cheap suit is described as being of a *couleur vite passée* ("quickly outdated color"). This I decided to translate as "colors that ran out of fashion," emphasizing the tawdriness of the garment by suggesting its inability even to hold its tint. In still another passage, a rich tourist in Saigon goes out on the town with a female escort, characterized as *une fine liane*, a slender "climbing vine" or "creeper." Both of those translations would convey perfectly well the slinky clinginess of the B-girl hanging onto her "Lord Jim," but I opted instead for *liana*, which, though less common in English, has the lilting and humanizing sonority of a woman's forename.

And one more example: in Jean Echenoz's novel *Big Blondes*, I ran up against the graffito *Ni dieu ni maître-nageur* (literally, "Neither god nor swimming instructor"), a pun on the well-known French anarchist slogan meaning "No gods, no masters." Unable to come up with a satisfactory solution in time for publication, I settled on *Neither Lord nor Swimming-Master*, playing off the phrase *lord and master*. The problem, of course, is that we don't have swimming *masters* in English, but *teachers*. Years later, offered a chance to revise, I changed it to *Those who can't do, teach swimming*. This is, admittedly, pure domestication, adapting Echenoz's very French graffito into something more Anglo-friendly. But unlike my first version, it also sounds, as it should, like the kind of sarcastic gibe that might actually be scrawled on the wall of a public pool, thereby fitting it more naturally into the novel's fictional world. Was this the best solution? As with Roche's *Compact* and Lê's *The Three Fates*, as with virtually every translation, there is no absolute answer to that question, only a series of choices to be made.

Such choices are the sinew and bone of a relatively new publishing phenomenon, the translator's memoir. Authored by such prominent practitioners as Gregory Rabassa, Mary Ann Caws, Edith Grossman, and Suzanne Jill Levine, and issued by comparatively large houses like New Directions and Yale University Press, these memoirs suggest a sea change in attitudes toward translations and those who make them. Whereas Reuben A. Brower's seminal 1959 anthology *On Translation* kicked off with: "Why a book on translation?" (followed by a defense of its own validity), recent titles suffer no such qualms. The fact that professional translators can place their musings with mainstream publishers is a clear indicator that hardly anyone asks that question anymore.

The late Gregory Rabassa, whose versions of Gabriel García Márquez, Julio Cortázar, Mario Vargas Llosa, and others helped to bring the Latin American Boom of the 1960s and 1970s to the United States, could be almost swaggering in his claims for the importance of the translator. Despite his profound respect for his authors, he refused to see himself as their subordinate, and assumed a stance of collaborator if not coauthor, one who grappled with the same materiality of language, the same problems of expression. And while his memoir, *If This Be Treason*, offers few guidelines for aspiring translators, and fewer still for those who like to fold practice into theoretical origami ("I leave strategy to the theorists as I confine myself to tactics," Rabassa writes),[2] it provides at least the illusion of a close-up glimpse of a master at work.

Especially engaging, to my mind, are his remarks on the famous opening of *One Hundred Years of Solitude*: "Muchos años después, frente al pelotón de fusilamiento, el coronel Aureliano Buendía había de recordar aquella tarde remota en que su padre lo llevó a conocer el hielo," which in Rabassa's translation became "Many years later, as he faced the firing squad, Colonel Aureliano Buendía was to remember that distant afternoon when his father took him to discover ice." "There are variant possibilities," Rabassa notes:

> *Había de* could have been *would* (How much wood can a woodchuck chuck?), but I think *was to* has a better feeling to it. I chose *remember* over *recall* because I feel that it conveys a deeper memory. *Remote* might have aroused thoughts of such inappropriate things as remote control and robots. Also, I liked *distant* when used with

time. ... The real problem for choice was with *conocer* and I have come to know that my selection has set a great many Professors Horrendo all aflutter. ... The word seen straight means to know a person or thing for the first time, to be familiar with something. What is happening here is a first-time meeting, or learning. It can also mean to know something more deeply than *saber*, to know from experience. García Márquez has used the Spanish word here with all its connotations. But *to know ice* just won't do in English. It implies, "How do you do, ice?" It could be "to experience ice." The first is foolish, the second is silly. When you get to know something for the first time, you've discovered it.[3]

Reading these memoirs, as well as various anthologies of essays about the art of translation, one notices how often certain preoccupations recur. Many stress the endless temptation to keep revising, even after publication. There are arguments pro and con regarding the importance of "compensation," the notion that if an effect can't be achieved where it occurs in the original, then it should be fitted in somewhere else. Some bring up the unpredictable share of subjectivity that goes into any rendering. "On Thursday, translating Moravia, [the translator] may write 'maybe,'" quips William Weaver, "and on Friday, translating Manzoni, he may write 'perhaps.'"[4] And though these books have their quota of wails and gnashing of teeth—translators, it seems, have always been a complaining lot—they also include many celebrations of the joy of engaging so intimately and creatively with an admired work.

Amid the thrills and spills are a number of practical questions as well. Should you read the source text before undertaking its translation? An incredulous "Of course!" might seem to be the only possible answer, and yet some translators choose to approach their assignments like blind dates—Rabassa, for instance, openly confesses to giving books their first reading while translating them. Cavalier or lazy as it may seem, this approach has its benefits: while strolling about backstage can help interpret the play, it can also lessen the sense of surprise that comes with fresh discovery. Must a translator stick to accepted usage? As noted above, translation tends to move language toward standard form, but there are times when a well-turned invention can neatly convey the author's rule breaking. My work with Maurice Roche, to take only one example, required many violations of "correct" English. Is a translation ever finished? As with any writing, endlessly finding further improvements comes with the territory, even after publication; something always slips by. The Italian and French words for this kind of second-guessing—*pentimenti, repentirs*—are indicative: the sense of a sin committed for which one must repent, that one profoundly regrets.

Minimizing those regrets is the translator's grail. Though it rarely happens, the ideal is to reread something one translated years ago and *not* find passages that cry out for improvement. One of my main strategies in this regard (not that it's infallible) is to begin with the words the author has given me, then envision the scene once I've sketched it out in English. Are those the words and phrases one would use to describe that couch, that hotel lobby, those characters' actions? Does this line of dialogue really sound like what someone would say in that circumstance? Is the tone right, the emphasis, the mood? And in order to make them right, do I need to alter the phrasing, syntax, or exact vocabulary? It's not a matter of changing the source text but rather of seeing what it conjures up, and then trying to re-create the same mental picture with the linguistic tools at my disposal—as opposed to feeling slavishly bound to a dictionary definition that might not say what I, or the original, need it to say. To arrive at a truth, sometimes you have to, as Dickinson intimated, "tell it slant."

Which leads to one of the most difficult questions facing translators: Should you (and how much should you) improve upon the original? The path from here to the age-old question of fidelity is obvious, and just as forked. Eliot Weinberger counsels "strictly avoiding" the temptation to improve, while others, such as John Rutherford, find it "perfectly reasonable" to better the original "because the target language is bound to offer expressive possibilities not available in the source language." Bellos, meanwhile, stresses the fuzziness of the line between "helping the reader" and "trashing the source."[5] Finding one's way, as ever, requires judgment and sensitivity. Like a good editor, a good translator needs to gauge which alterations will help the text best reach its destination and which are mere detours. The main thing is not to be waylaid by an artificial constraint that holds even glaring weaknesses in the original to be inviolate. "The worst mistake a translator can commit," warns William Weaver, "is to reassure himself by saying 'that's what it says in the original,' and renouncing the struggle to do his best."[6] The rough spots might be integral to the work, or they might be like splinters in a table, a flaw that the maker would gladly have sanded out. If an author mistakenly points us east when west is meant, or places a public monument in the wrong part of town (as with Kafka's bridge to Boston), is it a betrayal of the work or a service to it to quietly fix it in the translation? The living authors I've queried, when coming across such slips, have uniformly been grateful for the correction. But that's anecdotal, and no guarantee.

***

How to judge a translation? As we've seen, quite a few answers have been proposed over time. Taking translation as a practice, something done or performed, I would argue for criteria that focus on the success of execution or, again, on how convincing it is. Being bound by strict rules of meaning or even of consistency can sometimes be useful, but sometimes a well-placed deviation will produce a version that sings rather than stutters: even fidelity requires a bit of poetic license. More mysteriously still, two translations can be equally "accurate" in the strict sense, but one will plod while the other soars.

In this regard, I would contest Paul Ricoeur's assertion that "we would have to be able to compare the source and target texts with a third text which would bear the identical meaning that is supposed to be passed from the first to the second."[7] A translation is not a mirror image, but a work unto itself. Its audience is the target-language reader, and it is to that reader that the translation must speak. Even more than meaning, the translation must convey an atmosphere, an *aura* in the Benjaminian sense, that tells even readers wholly unversed in the source language that what they hold in their hands is true and representative.

The novelist and sometime translator André Gide denounced what he saw as pedantic and overly literal critiques that missed the point: "I deplore that spitefulness that tries to discredit a translation (perhaps excellent in other regards) because here and there slight mistranslations have slipped in. ... It is always easy to alert the public against very obvious errors, often mere trifles. The fundamental virtues are the hardest to appreciate and to point out."[8] The following case studies are meant not to discredit any given version (though I have my opinions), but rather to show the multiple ways in which different translators can go about rendering the same text.

To start with a personal example, Flaubert's unfinished last novel, *Bouvard and Pécuchet*, tells of two buffoonish middle-aged copy clerks who retire to the country and set out to conquer every endeavor known to humanity, from agriculture to romance. In one chapter, their explorations lead them (briefly) to try athletics, with the same disastrous results that greet every attempt. In this passage, Pécuchet tries out stilt walking:

> La nature semblait l'y avoir destiné, car il employa tout de suite le grand modèle, ayant des palettes à quatre pieds du sol, et, en équilibre là-dessus, il arpentait le jardin, pareil à une gigantesque cigogne qui se fût promenée.

This is from an anonymous translation published in 1904:

> Nature seemed to have destined him for [stilts], for he immediately made use of the great model with flat boards four feet from the ground, and, balanced thereon, he stalked over the garden like a gigantic stork taking exercise.

This is by T. W. Earp and G. W. Stonier, 1954:

> Nature seemed to have destined him for them, for he immediately used the large model, with treads four feet above the ground, and balancing on them, he stalked about the garden, like a gigantic crane out walking.

This is from A. J. Krailsheimer's version of 1976:

> Nature seemed to have destined him for that, for he at once used the large size, with footrests four feet above the ground, and balancing on them he strode up and down the garden, like some gigantic stork out for a walk.

And, for good measure, here is mine from 2005:

> Nature seemed to have predestined him for these. He immediately opted for the tallest model, with footrests four feet off the ground;

and, balancing up there, he paced around the garden like a giant stork out for its daily constitutional.

While each version shares many features with the others, what I tried to emphasize was the novel's pronounced comic effect, both by stressing the inordinate height of tall, skinny Pécuchet on those lengthy stilts (so *tallest* rather than *great* or *large*; *up there* rather than *on them*) and by the image of a stork on a W. C. Fieldsian *constitutional* rather than a mere *walk*.

That's a fairly straightforward example; this one is less so. Early in his career, Samuel Beckett translated a number of short Surrealist works, among them several passages from *The Immaculate Conception* (1930) by André Breton and Paul Éluard. Breton had served as a psychiatric intern during the First World War, and had been struck by the "astonishing imagery" of his mentally disturbed patients' verbal outpourings. Fourteen years later, he and Éluard tried to simulate the language and thought processes characteristic of those disorders.

In translation, the particular challenge of such a text is that it requires the translator not only to replicate the imagery but also to convey a realistic sense of the irrational logic underlying the mental states. Partly because of this challenge, such a text also provides an excellent object lesson in how the translator's subjective choices affect the result, and how a flash of inspiration can reveal hidden aspects of the original, or grant us access to it through a different door. Take the simulation of "General Paralysis":

> Ma grande adorée belle comme tout sur la terre et dans les plus belles étoiles de la terre que j'adore ma grande femme adorée par toutes les puissances des étoiles belle avec la beauté des milliards de reines qui parent la terre l'adoration que j'ai pour ta beauté me met à genoux

pour te supplier de penser à moi je me mets à tes genoux j'adore ta beauté …

The passage is by Éluard, its ardent, almost prayer-like tone characteristic of both his poetry and his love letters—and in fact, this text is written as a love letter.

Here's how it sounds from Richard Howard:

My great big adorable girl, beautiful as everything upon earth and in the most beautiful stars of the earth I adore, my great big girl adored by all the powers of the stars, lovely with the beauty of the billions of queens that adorn the earth, my adoration for your beauty brings me to my knees to beg you to think of me, I throw myself at your knees, I adore your beauty …

and it's signed "Yours in a torch." Which is fine as far as it goes, though to my ear it makes for a rather jocular interpretation, as if Éluard were being read by Cary Grant.

Beckett, for his part, takes an anachronistic approach that connects two poetic traditions as if by FireWire:

Thou my great one whom I adore beautiful as the whole earth and in the most beautiful stars of the earth that I adore thou my great woman adored by all the powers of the stars beautiful with the beauty of the thousands of millions of queens who adorn the earth the adoration that I have for thy beauty brings me to my knees to beg thee to think of me I am brought to my knees I adore thy beauty …

signed "Thine in flames." Without belaboring the issue, I'll simply note that by transposing the discourse of a general paralytic from 1930 into the heraldic idiom of courtly love lyrics, Beckett has come closer to preserving the essence of Éluard's feverish entreaty than Howard, even though Howard actually hews closer to the strict meaning of the original.

That said, there are times when the translator's sense of invention can run amok, yielding an interesting Oulipian exercise, at best, but not much else. One scholar proposes translating not for meaning or sound but for appearance—so that, for instance, the English noun *soul* should be translated by the French adjective *soûl* ("drunk"). Another, Clive Scott, breaks the text into dislocated shreds. Presenting translation as a process that tends "to transform the transdicted into the transcripted,"[9] Scott has his way with Apollinaire's unrequited-love poem "Annie" (from *Alcools*), the first two stanzas of which read in French as:

> Sur la côte du Texas
> Entre Mobile et Galveston il y a
> Un grand jardin tout plein de roses
> Il contient aussi une villa
>
> Qui est une grande rose
> Une femme se promène souvent
> Dans le jardin toute seule
> Et quand je passe sur la route bordée de tilleuls
> Nous nous regardons

Here's my fairly straightforward translation:

> On the Texas coast
> Between Mobile and Galveston there is
> A large garden full of roses
> And inside it a villa
> That is a giant rose
>
> Oftentimes a woman walks
> Through that garden on her own
> And when I pass on that linden-lined street
> Our eyes meet

And here's Scott's version:

OntheTexasseaboard

La mer,

    cigarette?

Comme tu tremblais!

    Comme tu te serrais contre moi!

On aurait dit que tu me prenais pour un . . .

    Le transistor s'est arrêté.

between

M-O-B-I-L-E   and   Galvestonthere's

A   large   garden

brimming with   roses

andthere's

a   villa, too,   itself

a   giantrose

Often

A   WomanWalks

Quite alone

SATURDAY EVENING POST SATURDAY EVENING POST SATURDAY EVENING POST
/ SATUR

and whenIpassbyon the limetreelinedroad WE

Look at each other . . .

Having "recourse ... to a certain centrifugality of layout and to vertical syntagmatic decoys," Scott proposes that his "halting, tentative" version performs "the existential predicament explored by the poem"[10]—which is all well and good but, as Richard Bentley might have said, he must not call it Apollinaire. The fake intimacy of the interjected French lines, like the soundtrack of some PBS-standard foreign flick, replete with anachronistic transistor radio, clashes with the scene's outside-looking-in wistfulness. Apart from which, Apollinaire's poem does quite enough existential soul- (or *soûl-*) searching without the typographical pyrotechnics, thank you very much.

This is not to say that translators should avoid imaginative leaps and stick to the grid. Far from it: Beckett's heraldic transposition is only a small sample of how this can work to advantage, and I have tried to show many other examples in this book of translators acting as creative partners. The field is wide open, and there's ample room for the translator's personality to coexist, cohabit, even commingle with the author's. I would even submit that this kind of semifusion is necessary if the translation is to have any personality at all. In the best of cases, author and translator enter into a two-way engagement (whether literal or imaginary), conspiring to yield a translation with all the effect and staying power of the original. Suzanne Jill Levine, in *The Subversive Scribe*, details how she adapted for English speakers the wordplay and idiosyncrasies of her Latin American authors in tandem with those authors, with all the collaborative reinvention that entails. But regardless of the author's involvement, the process remains similar: "I don't become the author when I'm translating his prose or poetry," the poet Paul Blackburn told an interviewer, "but I'm certainly getting my talents into his hang-ups. Another person's preoccupations are occupying me. ... It's not just a matter of reading the language and understanding it and putting it into English. It's understanding something that makes the man do it, where he's going. ... It's not just understanding the text. In a way you live it each time, I mean, *you're there.*"[11]

The difference between, say, the extra dimension that Beckett brings to Éluard and the demolition job Scott inflicts on Apollinaire is that one enriches our experience of the original by bringing out aspects we might not have suspected while the other merely grandstands, hopping up and down for the camera and drowning out the author's voice. A good translation, created by a thoughtful and talented translator, aims not to betray the original but to honor it by offering something of equal—possibly even greater—beauty in its name. A good translation aims to enhance and refresh, not to denature, not to obscure, not to petrify.

7   Verse and Controverse

"For a poet, translating is like devouring one's own brains," wrote Anna Akhmatova.[1] Though her terms might have been more ghoulish than most, she was expressing a common attitude: that for many poets, translation is the great bane. They dread that some clunky wordsmith will either run roughshod over their meter and rhyme or else adhere to them so doggedly that the airborne original becomes a leaden, earthbound thing. If the Bible provided scholarly translation with the primary battleground for its holy wars, for many years now the bone of contention among humanists has been verse. Poetry—precisely "what gets lost in translation," according to Robert Frost's pithy, much-misquoted gibe[2]—remains for many the ultimate test of a translator's mettle, not only because its technical features and concision leave little room for error but also because the genre has long held an unassailable position at the crest of the literary hill. (Until the seventeenth century, those spoiling for a fight about translation had as their choices the sacred texts and classical poetry; literary prose in the modern sense barely existed, and in any case was strictly infra dig.)

"The prose writer, the novelist, the philosopher, can be translated, and often are, without too much damage," Paul Valéry

advanced rather snottily, but "a true poet is strictly untranslatable." And yet it has often been true poets themselves who
have produced the most beautiful and enduring translations
of verse, in some cases renderings so intensely personal as to
break through the constraints that would limit them.* "The great
translations," observed Kenneth Rexroth, "survive into our time
because ... the translator's act of identification was so complete
that he spoke with the veridical force of his own utterance, conscious of communicating directly to his own audience." Such
translations soar beyond strict considerations of form—considerations that have long dominated the debate over whether
poetry is or is not translatable, and that ultimately mire it in
technicalities.[3]

The reason why technicalities enter into the debate so read-
ily is no mystery: more than with any other type of literature,
the substance of poetry is tightly bound with its formal properties, regardless of how "free" the verse purports to be. (The
rhythms and cadences of Walt Whitman, or e. e. cummings, are
no less considered and purposeful than those of Milton.) And
this immediately embroils the translator in a unique set of questions regarding rhyme, meter, and genre, as well as what those

---

* Indeed, Alexander Tytler believed that "none but a poet can translate
a poet." A very short shortlist of such poets—limiting the scope to twen-
tieth- and twenty-first-century Anglophones, and leaving out those al-
ready mentioned in the introduction—would include David Antin, Mary
Jo Bang, Paul Blackburn, Robert Bly, Anne Carson, John Ciardi, James
Dickey, Robert Duncan, David Gascoyne, Donald Hall, Seamus Heaney,
Richard Howard, Galway Kinnell, Kenneth Koch, Stanley Kunitz, Rika
Lesser, Denise Levertov, James Merrill, W. S. Merwin, Edna St. Vincent
Millay, Ron Padgett, Robert Pinsky, Adrienne Rich, May Sarton, Charles
Simic, May Swenson, Nathaniel Tarn, Allen Tate, Charles Tomlinson,
Eliot Weinberger, Richard Wilbur, W. C. and C. K. Williams ...

genres mean, rhetorically and culturally, between two languages. When translating a sonnet from French to English, should you retain the twelve syllables per line common in French prosody, or transpose to the more familiar ten of the English tradition? What to do about the deployment of "masculine" and "feminine" rhymes, or indeed about rhyme at all? Some translators retain at least some sort of rhyme scheme, even if the meaning has to be altered somewhat, while others find blank or free verse a less compromising medium in the target. In my own case, I've had the disorienting experience, when translating poems by Baudelaire, Rimbaud, and Proust, of starting out in free verse and having the English text, like the planchette on a Ouija board, move me inexorably toward at least some use of rhyme.

(That said, let's not lean too heavily on the distinction between poetry and prose, or their relative levels of stylistic difficulty. When Flaubert rhapsodized about inventing a writing style "as rhythmical as verse and as precise as science," he meant merely that he wanted to infuse prose with the same values as those traditionally ascribed to poetry. "As soon as a novel becomes as well written as poetry," writes Adam Thirlwell, "as soon as style is everything, then the translation of a novel becomes not a peripheral problem, but a central one"[4]—becomes, in other words, just as thorny for fiction as for a sonnet. We'll leave aside for the moment that no translation of a literary text is ever a peripheral problem.)

The writer and critic Edouard Roditi, who translated Yaşar Kemal's *Memed, My Hawk*, wrote that "the spirit of poetry resides entirely in its body; the more carefully a translator observes all the linguistic, grammatical, rhetorical and narrative details of a poem, the more truly he renders its spirit when he meticulously reconstructs its body in another language." This is, on the surface of it, an honorable proposition, one that would respect the integrity of form and content. Very often, however, it leads to wooden re-creations of a lively original, and W. S. Merwin is no doubt closer to the truth when he cautions that the formal elements of poetry "are embedded in the original language. … You can suggest, you can torment your own language into repeating them, but even if you do, you're not going to get the form doing in your language what it did in the original." Language changes, usage changes, and so do readers' ways of receiving a text. The classical meters of old, if reproduced in the modern context, quickly lose their stateliness to become merely, in Yves Bonnefoy's words, "faked or dispirited regularity." Merwin again: "I have to feel that I have a sense of what makes that poem exciting in the original. I don't want to mislead about the real meaning of the poem. But I want it to be a poem that has that same kind of—I don't know—drama, that same kind of … urgency. It won't be exactly the urgency. But if it doesn't have any urgency, if it's flat, it doesn't matter whether it rhymes or has meter or anything. You've lost the poem."[5]

To some extent, the argument can be situated between translators (or poets who translate) and poets who consider themselves exclusively "source" authors, for whom the exact characteristics of their poems are not to be tampered with. The Russian poet Joseph Brodsky expressed this intransigence to Merwin when he declared that "Russian poetry is sacred," meaning that meter and rhyme must be scrupulously preserved in translation. ("Oh sure, just like all other poetry," replied Merwin, unimpressed.) Without revisiting what I've already said about giving translations voice and flavor, I'll simply add that this seems to go double for poetry, where the very concentration and formalism of the genre demands even greater investment of poetic sensibility to keep the work alive. The translator Clarence Brown noted that translators of "poetic distinction" ultimately translate not into the target language but into a language of their own. "Mandelstam ... translated Petrarch not into Russian, but into Mandelstam. ... [Robert] Lowell does not translate into English, but into Lowell."[6]

***

In 1992, the scholar Douglas Robinson, reaching back to the ur-debate between saints, traced out two distinct lineages: an "impersonal, perfectionist, and systematic" one descended from Augustine, and a series of "mavericks"—such as Ezra Pound, Robert Lowell, and Vladimir Nabokov—descended from Jerome. As Robinson noted of the latter group, "one of the great temptations of mainstream Western translatology" has been to eliminate these "quirky, crotchety hotheads" from the gene pool.[7]

Pound would no doubt top pretty much anyone's list of quirky hotheads. Deeply rooted in American "kulchur" and its idioms, he nonetheless did more than almost any other poet of his time to incorporate vast swaths of lyrical tradition from myriad languages and epochs into the grand current of modern American verse, revitalizing that current as he went. Like Goethe, he believed in the power of translation to energize the target culture, arguing that "a great age of literature is perhaps always a great age of translations; or follows it."[8] And just as Pound, a prodigious mimic, drew on snippets of world literature to shape and inform his own work, the epic *Cantos* being the most notable example, so he combed through vast literary resources for his translations, at times adapting archaic English phrasings to convey the archaisms of Italian poets such as Cavalcanti, at others adopting a neutral modern diction to suggest antiquity through timelessness.

No doubt one of Pound's most contentious translation efforts remains his versions of classical Chinese poems, published in the 1915 volume *Cathay*. According to the subtitle, the collection was adapted *for the Most Part from the Chinese of Rihaku* [Li Po], *from the Notes of the Late Ernest Fenollosa, and the Decipherings of the Professors Mori and Ariga*. The fact that Pound knew "less than nothing of Chinese" (in the words of Kenneth Rexroth, who nevertheless deemed *Cathay* Pound's finest work),[9] and relied instead on Fenollosa's scholarship and his own instincts, has drawn scornful harrumphs from a century's worth of critics, but no doubt it also accounts largely for the moving delicacy of his renderings. Let the pedants yowl: many are they who feel Pound captured the spirit of Li Po and Confucius far more closely and gracefully than the rows of professors hewing to their ideograms. Indeed, one of the celebrated paradoxes of translation is that these free adaptations in some ways ended up being more literal than many learned versions; at least one scholar has demonstrated that, despite Pound's lack of Chinese, he "*intuitively* corrected mistakes in the Fenollosa manuscript."[10]

Let's put this intuition to the test. One of the most celebrated poems in *Cathay* is "The River Merchant's Wife: A Letter." Before considering Pound's translation of the poem, and a few other, more "faithful," ones, we'll start with his source, the crib by Fenollosa:

> My hair was at first covering my brows
> Breaking flower branches I was frolicking in front of our gate.
> When you came riding on bamboo stilts
> And going about my seat, you played with the blue plums.
> Together we dwelt in the same Chokan village.
> And we two little ones had neither mutual dislike or suspicion. (no evil thoughts or bashfulness)

At fourteen I became your wife—
Bashful I never opened my face (I never laughed)
but lowering my head I always faced toward a dark wall ashamed to
    see anybody—she sat in dark corners
And though a thousand times called, not once did I look around ...

At fifteen I first opened my brows
(i.e., I first knew what married life meant now she opens her
    eyebrows.
i.e.. smooths out the wrinkles between her brows. She now began to
    understand love, and to be happy.)
And so I desired to live and die with you even after death, I wish to
    be with you even as dust, and even as ashes—partially together.
I always had in me the faith of holding to pillars
And why should I think of climbing the husband looking out terrace.

At 16, however, you had to go far away.
(both *yen* & *yo* are adj. expressing form of water passing over hidden
    rocks)
(towards Shoku passing through the difficult place of Yentotai at
    Kuto.)
The ship must be careful of them in May.
Monkeys cry sorrowful above heaven.

Your footsteps, made by your reluctant departure, in front of our gate
    one by one have been grown up into green moss.
These mosses have grown so deep that it is difficult to wipe them
    away.
And the fallen leaves indicate autumn wind which (to my thought
    only) appears to come earlier than usual.
It being already August, the butterflies are yellow.
And yellow as they are, they fly in pairs on the western garden grass.
Affected by this, (absence) my heart pains.
The longer the absence lasts, the deeper I mourn, my early fine pink
    face, will pass to oldness, to my great regret.
If you be coming down as far as the Three Narrows sooner or later,
Please let me know by writing
For I will go out to meet, not saying that the way be far,
And will directly come to Chofusha.

From these notes, Pound made this:

> While my hair was still cut straight across my forehead
> I played about the front gate, pulling flowers.
> You came by on bamboo stilts, playing horse,
> You walked about my seat, playing with blue plums.
> And we went on living in the village of Chōkan:
> Two small people, without dislike or suspicion.
>
> At fourteen I married My Lord you.
> I never laughed, being bashful.
> Lowering my head, I looked at the wall.
> Called to, a thousand times, I never looked back.
>
> At fifteen I stopped scowling,
> I desired my dust to be mingled with yours
> Forever and forever, and forever.
> Why should I climb the look out?
>
> At sixteen you departed
> You went into far Ku-tō-en, by the river of swirling eddies,
> And you have been gone five months.
> The monkeys make sorrowful noise overhead.
>
> You dragged your feet when you went out.
> By the gate now, the moss is grown, the different mosses,
> Too deep to clear them away!
> The leaves fall early this autumn, in wind.
> The paired butterflies are already yellow with August
> Over the grass in the West garden;
> They hurt me. I grow older.
> If you are coming down through the narrows of the river Kiang,
> Please let me know beforehand,
> And I will come out to meet you
> As far as Chō-fū-Sa.

Limiting ourselves to the final lines of the poem, here is a version by the poet Witter Bynner from 1929:

And now, in the Eighth-month, yellowing butterflies
Hover, two by two, in our west-garden grasses. ...
And, because of all this, my heart is breaking
And I fear for my bright cheeks, lest they fade.
Oh, at last, when you return through the three Pa districts,
Send me a message home ahead!
And I will come and meet you and will never mind the distance,
All the way to Chang-fêng Sha.

and a more recent one (1976) by Wai-lim Yip, who numbers the stanzas as if they were mathematical propositions:

23. In the eighth month, butterflies come
24. In pairs over the grass in the West Garden.
25. These smite my heart.
26. I sit down worrying and youth passes away.
27. When eventually you would come down from the Three Gorges.
28. Please let me know ahead of time.
29. I will meet you, no matter how far,
30. Even all the way to Long Wind Sand.

While it is hardly making it new to say that Pound's is more expressive, more like the letter that a pining young wife would, in fact, write to her absent husband, there are two notable facts that emerge from comparing these versions. One has to do with economy, how much more Pound says with less, and how this affects the reading experience. Rather than spell out the distance the merchant's wife is willing to travel for a brief reunion (Bynner's *never mind the distance*, Yip's *no matter how far*), Pound simply lets the phrase *As far as Chō-fū-Sa* spell it out for him. Western readers likely don't know how far Chō-fū-Sa actually is, but we know that it's far enough, and by keeping it simple, Pound invites us into the intimacy of that shared knowledge. The second has to do with the use of place-names. As with Patrick Modiano's precise enumerations of obscure Parisian sites,

Pound here creates a sense of "Chineseness" that makes no untoward demands of finely crafted English usage—unlike Yip, whose slightly stilted syntax and artificially translated locales makes the poem feel more foreign and distant, and therefore less impactful, because less real: we can believe that a place in China is called Chō-fū-Sa, but not Long Wind Sand (just as in France, one might visit the town of Eaubonne, but not Goodwater). Taking our cue from George Steiner, we can say that Pound created not the more accurate rendition but the better illusion, one that adheres more closely than other versions to our Western conception of what Chinese poetry is. Writes Steiner, "Pound can imitate and persuade with utmost economy not because he or his reader knows so much but because both concur in knowing so little"[11]—recalling Eliot's famous characterization of Pound as "the inventor of Chinese poetry for our time."

Pound himself made no claim to fidelity—we are, after all, talking about the man who named a Confucian protagonist "Hep-Cat Chung" and gave Sextus Propertius a Frigidaire—preferring instead to concentrate not on "what a man sez, but wot he *means* ... the *implication* of the word."[12] In this regard, "The River Merchant's Wife" certainly contains its share of liberties and insertions—in the first two stanzas alone, comparing Pound's version with his source notes, we can highlight *still cut straight, pulling flowers, playing horse, My Lord you*—but each of these helps create a linguistic world both reminiscent of the one evoked by Li Po and emitting a freshness all its own. As with Mandelstam and Lowell in Clarence Brown's example, Pound ultimately translated into Pound.

An equally controversial book is Lowell's *Imitations*, which has been dividing readers since its publication sixty years ago. Stating from the outset that he has "dropped lines, moved lines, moved stanzas, changed images and altered meter and intent," Lowell defended his approach to translation on the grounds that what he dismissively called the "reliable" method "gets the literal meaning but misses the tone, and ... in poetry tone is of course everything." In this, Lowell was echoing translators such as Edward FitzGerald and the seventeenth-century English poet Abraham Cowley, who prefaced his translations of Pindar by noting, "I have left out, and added what I please; nor make it so much my aim to let the reader know precisely what [Pindar] spake, as what was his *way* and *manner* of speaking."[13]

Not surprisingly, what the critic D. S. Carne-Ross called Lowell's propensity to "take possession of the original and dominate it" attracted its share of critics. One commentator railed against Lowell for having, in one translation, made Anna Akhmatova "say things profoundly offensive to her memory" and, in another, turned François Villon into "Mickey Spillane." Lowell himself, however, viewed his work more as a way of honoring the creative possibilities inherent in translation, and his own remarks suggest respect rather than domination. "The whole point of translating," he told Carne-Ross, "is to bring into English something that didn't exist in English before."[14]

As it happens, both Lowell and Pound had a go at Arthur Rimbaud's poem "Au cabaret vert," and it is enlightening to compare the results. First, in a more literal version (by Wallace Fowlie, whose translations epitomize the "reliable" sort Lowell kicks against), the poem reads:

> For a week my boots had been torn
> By the pebbles on the roads. I was getting into Charleroi.
> —At the Cabaret-Vert: I asked for bread
> And butter, and for ham that would be half chilled.

Happy, I stretched out my legs under the green
Table. I looked at the very naïve subjects
Of the wallpaper.—And it was lovely,
When the girl with huge tits and lively eyes,

—She's not one to be afraid of a kiss!—
Laughing brought me bread and butter,
Warm ham, in a colored plate.

Lowell, less concerned with scene setting than with Rimbaud's youthful bravado—his tone—strikes a more casual note by introducing bits of slang not found in the original:

For eight days I had been knocking my boots
on the road stones. I was entering Charleroi.
At the Green Cabaret, I called for ham,
half cold, and a large helping of tartines.

Happy, I kicked my shoes off, cooled my feet
under the table, green like the room, and laughed
at the naïve Belgian pictures on the wall.
But it was terrific when the house-girl

with her earth-mother tits and come-on eyes—
no Snow Queen having cat-fits at a kiss—
brought me tarts and ham on a colored plate.

Pound, finally, emphasizes Rimbaud's teenage impatience by stripping the poem to its essentials, while nonetheless preserving flashes of a rhyme scheme:

Wearing out my shoes, 8th day
On the bad roads, I got into Charleroi.
Bread, butter, at the Green Cabaret
And the ham half cold.

Got my legs stretched out
And was looking at the simple tapestries,
Very nice when the gal with the big bubs
And lively eyes,

Not one to be scared of a kiss and more,
Brought the butter and bread with a grin
And the luke-warm ham on a colored plate.

By shedding syllables like so much scurf, Pound's version stresses the sense of urgency, even in repose, that characterizes Rimbaud's road songs. The language here is reduced almost to shorthand—a far cry from the original's alexandrines, and yet appropriate: if Rimbaud were alive today, he might very well write rock songs (think Jim Carroll or Patti Smith) instead of sonnets.

***

But is it translation? At the other end of the spectrum waits the glowering visage of the self-styled "Vladimir Adamant Nabokov," the dean of nondeviationists, swishing his Augustinian hick'ry stick at rascally Hieronymites like Pound and Lowell. "We must dismiss, once and for all the conventional notion that a translation 'should read smoothly' and 'should not sound like a translation,' " he wrote. "In point of fact, any translation that does *not* sound like a translation is bound to be inexact upon inspection; while, on the other hand, the only virtue of a good translation is faithfulness and completeness." In the frequently cited opening of his poem "On Translating *Eugene Onegin*" (1954), Nabokov skewered "this pathetic business of translating":

What is translation? On a platter
A poet's pale and glaring head,
A parrot's screech, a monkey's chatter,
And profanation of the dead.

Earlier, he identified the three deadly sins of translation: ignorance, omission, and, worst of all, "vilely beautifying" a masterpiece to suit public taste—"a crime, to be punished by the stocks, as plagiarists were in the shoebuckle days."[15]

Nabokov's reputation as modern translation's most stiff-necked schoolmarm was not earned lightly, and rests on such inflexible pronouncements as "The clumsiest literal translation is a thousand times more useful than the prettiest paraphrase" and "I want translations with copious footnotes, footnotes reaching up like skyscrapers to the top of this or that page so as to leave only the gleam of one textual line between commentary and eternity." This he wanted and this he got in his translation of Pushkin's epic *Eugene Onegin*—the "greatest poem in the Russian language," according to Nabokov—on which he labored for decades and which he eventually published in 1964 in no fewer than four volumes, including twelve hundred pages of commentary. (With characteristic brilliance, Nabokov lampooned his own approach in the concurrently written novel *Pale Fire*.) His foreword to *Onegin* seems designed to scare off those seeking an easy read: "To my ideal of literalism I sacrificed everything (elegance, euphony, clarity, good taste, modern usage, and even grammar) that the dainty mimic prizes higher than truth." And, with a turn of phrase that would have made R. H. Horne proud: "It is when the translator sets out to render the 'spirit,' and not the mere sense of the text, that he begins to traduce his author."[16]

Yet his stance was not always so pugnacious, and if we look farther back, we find a kinder, gentler Nabokov producing many rhymed and metered translations. Among these is a partial early translation of *Onegin* from 1945, in which he indulged in the same "crimes" that he would later prosecute so acidly:

Diana's bosom, Flora's dimple
are very charming, I agree—

but there's a greater charm, less simple,
—the instep of Terpsichore.
By prophesying to the eye
a prize with which no prize can vie
'tis a fair token and a snare
for swarms of daydreams. Everywhere ...

—a translation that turns out to be not so very different from, though less effective than, the one by Babette Deutsch, then commonly available in the 1936 Modern Library edition of Pushkin's collected works:

Diana's breast, the face of Flora,
Are charming, friends, but I would put
Them both aside and only for a
Glimpse of Terpsichore's sweet foot.
Prophetic of a priceless pleasure,
A clue to joys beyond all measure ...

And this might in fact be the point: if the best Nabokov could offer was an inferior version of what already existed, it hardly seemed worth the effort. Better to effect an about-face and take a stance so extreme that no one else could touch it.

The turning point occurred in the 1950s, when Nabokov stopped writing prose in Russian and switched to American—a switch that, as he openly recognized, occasioned a certain amount of distress: "My private tragedy," he wrote in 1958, "which cannot, indeed should not, be anybody's concern, is that I had to abandon my natural language, my natural idiom, my rich, infinitely rich and docile Russian tongue, for a second-rate brand of English."[17] Not coincidentally, this was also when Nabokov, like his equally nostalgic compatriot Brodsky, began taking a hard line about the "sacredness" of Russian verse. By the time he published his final, revised version of *Onegin*, in 1975, he had recast the above passage as:

> Diana's bosom, Flora's cheeks,
> are charming, dear friends!
> However, the little foot of Terpsichore
> is for me in some way more charming.
> By prophesying to the gaze
> an unpriced recompense,
> with token beauty it attracts
> the willful swarm of longings.

Nabokov justified this sea change on the grounds that Pushkin's rhyme, rhythm, and allusions can be brought over only by means of the most exact transcription, propped up with copious annotations. In this, he was responding to the common notion that Pushkin has a particularly hard time surviving translation into English, as even the middlebrow culture purveyor *Time* magazine recognized: "Russia's Shakespeare does not travel well. … Most Western readers, confronted by examples of Pushkin's genius, can only nod politely—or, in the case of the worst translations, nod off."[18]

The problem with Nabokov's revised *Onegin* is that, in trying so hard to restore this genius for Westerners, it offers less an artistic experience than a "Tell, don't show" exercise. Not only has this version been bleached of its earlier cousin's *élan* and been made to sound more like an after-dinner speech than a great Russian epic, there also seems to be little gained by way of "completeness of meaning," the putative reason for such sacrifices. Ultimately *Onegin* is translated not into English, even colorless literal English, but into substandard Nabokov. What the final version does afford, with its painstaking annotations, is a deeper understanding of Pushkin's creative process, and of Nabokov's own process (and no doubt his psyche) as well. But what we lose in this translation is, precisely, the poetry.

Such has been the opinion of many, including, with no pretense of originality, myself. The Russian scholar Alexander Gerschenkron memorably and damningly adjudged that Nabokov's translation "can and indeed should be studied, but despite all the cleverness and occasional brilliance it cannot be read." And the poet Dudley Fitts called Nabokov's predilection for mountainous footnotes "endearing" but hardly viable: "We need something at once less ambitious and more audacious: another poem. ... [The translator] must be a poet as well as an interpreter. To put it more bluntly, his interpretation must be an act of poetry." In fact, Fitts's bluntness echoes Nabokov's own early assertion that a translator "must have as much talent, or at least the same kind of talent, as the author he chooses ... [and] must possess the gift of mimicry"—a gift he later derided ("the dainty mimic").[19]

Among the many critiques of Nabokov's latter-day approach, the bluntest and most memorable came from his longtime compadre Edmund Wilson, who had hailed his earlier renderings of Pushkin as "the best translations of poetry of any kind," but who laid into the 1964 *Onegin* in a damning essay for the *New York Review of Books*. Beginning by calling the translation "something of a disappointment" and ending with a disparaging assessment of both Nabokov's English and his grasp of Russian, via frequent digs at the "overdone" commentary, Wilson left little intact of either the translation or the two men's friendship. Nabokov, wounded and insulted, responded in kind, inaugurating an escalating exchange that mixed dueling erudition with personal slight, and that quickly outstripped any considerations of translation theory or practice. In a "reply to his critics," he doubled down by asserting that his version's only shortcoming was to be

"still not close enough and not ugly enough," a flaw he made
sure to repair in the 1975 revised edition.[20]

As the tempest was winding down, Isaiah Berlin offered Wilson his own appraisal: "The point to make, I am sure, is that the
translation as such is nothing but a curiosity of literature ... that
[Nabokov] has all the faults of a self-intoxicated virtuoso with
a vast narcissistic talent and no capacity for conveying other
works of art. ... The whole thing is part of the work of Nabokov
and not of Pushkin."[21] Needless to say, one could, with only a
small swerve of the imagination, apply a similar judgment to
such enduring, and by now much more accepted, efforts as
Pope's *Iliad*, Pound's *Cathay*, and Lowell's *Imitations*.

8   On the Fringe

There are reasons galore why translation should seem impossible, a pale shadow, "Cheate bread." Some betrayal, some departure from the source text, will always elicit the ancient *nay*. And yet, among the most solid citizens of "our" literature, works that are now in our cultural mainstream, quite a few arrived as immigrants, established a homestead, and flourished. Translation might be impossible in principle, but in practice it seems to manage just fine. Still, there are certain provinces of the literary map in which translation has encountered rockier footpaths, and it raises the question, can everything be translated?

My toss-the-baby-in-the-deep-end experience with Maurice Roche's *CodeX* (see chapter 6) taught me early on that even the thorniest linguistic problems can be solved, at least theoretically (though I have yet to solve a number of Roche's). It's true that a translator from English would have a hard time preserving the prepositional enigmas of "upset" and "setup," or "cutting down" a tree and then "cutting it up"; or the sight-sound disparity of "laughter" and "slaughter"; or any amount of wordplay that our language, like all languages, makes possible. Fans of popular music, from Cole Porter to the French singer-poet Georges Brassens to the Groucho Marx signature tune "Lydia, the Tattooed

Lady," know how heavily songs—not to mention humor—lean on a complex interplay of rhymes, rhythms, meanings, and cultural peculiarities. Yet even these, in the right hands, have sometimes come alive in other languages. "The only impossible things in translation are those that haven't been done," contends David Bellos, who takes the affirming stance that "when you have to pay attention to more than one dimension of an utterance—when your mind is engaged in multilevel pattern-matching pursuits—you find resources in your language you never knew were there."[1] In the following examples, I aim to show how even "impossible" originals have, in fact, found their way into other languages, sometimes with as much inventiveness and individualism as the original itself.

Georges Perec's lipogrammatic novel *La disparition* (1969), for one, was long considered untranslatable because it contains not a single instance of the letter *e*, in French as in English the most common letter—so much so that Perec, in those pre-search-and-replace days, reportedly glued a tack to the *e* key of his typewriter as a painful guarantor against letting one sneak in. But in 1995, Gilbert Adair published his English version, the equally *e*-less *A Void*, which contains many adroit substitutions and adaptations, including his shift of a composition by Baudelaire (or Baudlair) into stanzas by his spiritual twin Po.

Similarly, Raymond Roussel, though considered a quintessentially "difficult" author—his writings inspired the Surrealists, the Nouveau Roman, the New York School, and the Oulipo, of which Perec was a member—is in fact quite enjoyable both to read and to translate. His matter-of-fact descriptions of outlandish creations (such as the fluid mechanics of a giant earthworm "playing" the zither by selectively releasing droplets of heavy water, or a cluster of grapes whose flesh contains complex dioramas) can be exhilarating, while the bravura stylistic performance of his prose offers up linguistic beauties—through concision, precision, musicality—even within the formal constraints the author imposed on himself.

These constraints are what have primarily, and unfairly, placed Roussel among the ranks of the "untranslatables." In many of his works, the 1910 novel *Impressions of Africa* being a prime example, the episodes, conceits, and details from which Roussel fashions his characters and their actions were determined not by authorial whimsy but by a highly regulated process—Roussel's celebrated "method"—in which language itself is the sole motor and guide, and in which moment after moment hinges on highly complex puns. For instance, the Luenn'chetuz, the coronation dance performed by King Talou's wives that results in copious belching, was generated by a dual interpretation of the phrase *théorie à renvois*: both a treatise (*théorie*) with annotations (*renvois*)—in this case, Talou's proclamation of his own sovereignty—and a procession (*théorie*) involving burps (*renvois*). Another episode was derived from the name and address of Roussel's shoemaker, Hellstern, 5 Place Vendome, which, mutated into the homophonic string of words *helice tourne zinc plat de rend dome* ("propeller turns zinc flat goes dome"), inspired the apparatus built by one of the novel's characters.

It sounds daunting, but in reality, Roussel kept his linguistic procedure—his most inventive apparatus of all—scrupulously hidden from sight, and stepped out from behind the curtain only in the posthumously published memoir *How I Wrote Certain of My Books* (1935). Since none of the author's intricate scaffolding was visible to his French readers, for me as translator it meant that trying to replicate that scaffolding in English was unnecessary, even if important to keep in mind. In fact, the bigger challenge I faced with *Impressions of Africa* lay in maintaining the original's concision and humor. My task was to squeeze as much linguistic wonder as I could into as few words as possible, as Roussel had done. The means by which he got there was his secret.

Method and derivation take equal prominence in the works of Roussel's devoted fans the Surrealists. André Breton stated early on that "Language has been given to man so that he may make Surrealist use of it," and the Surrealists did indeed make free use of the linguistic resources offered by their native tongue—what Breton, with reference to Marcel Duchamp's verbal play, called "words mak[ing] love."[2] Among these resources is the fact that French usually puts its modifiers after the noun. Particularly in the case of automatic writing, composed very quickly and without conscious control, it leaves the poet the blink of an eye in which to careen from the expected path into a wholly different direction. So, for example, a *brosse à dents* (toothbrush) could, in the rush of spontaneous generation, easily morph into a *brosse à danse* (dancebrush) or a *brosse à danger* (dangerbrush). The problem in English is that we often, though not always, have to start with the modifier, effectively anticipating the surprise transformation before it's even a surprise.

One solution to this, as in the case of Roussel, is to forget about how the original was created and consider an automatic text similar to any other piece of writing, regardless of its genesis and internal logic—for like any piece of writing, it tries to create and transmit to the reader a cluster of meanings and sensations. The electric charge of these works, in the original as, we hope, in translation, derives from the reaction between words, between bits of language, as if between positive and negative particles—which means, somewhat paradoxically, that they are more likely to retain their potency the less the translator tries to "reproduce" the automatic experience in the target version. Will it always work? Of course not, but given the complex underpinnings of many of these writings, the success rate has been surprisingly high. And, as it does in the composition of automatic texts, serendipity occasionally comes to the translator's aid. Breton's poem "Tournesol" (Sunflower), one of his most anthologized works, contains the stanza:

Une ferme prospérait en plein Paris
Et ses fenêtres donnaient sur la voie lactée
Mais personne ne l'habitait encore à cause des *survenants*
Des survenants qu'on sait plus dévoués que les *revenants*

The mechanism of these lines pivots on visual and auditory wordplay, in this case the transition from *survenant*, literally a person who arrives unexpectedly, and *revenant*, a spirit; we can almost reconstruct Breton's mental process as he wrote this poem, with one word very naturally suggesting its near-homonym as his pen traced the line of verse. What is one to do with a passage like this in English? In this case, for once, the answer is so simple it nearly falls into the translator's lap—and in fact several translators have independently resorted to it, as I do here:

A farm prospered in the heart of Paris
Its windows gave onto the Milky Way
But no one lived there because of the *guests*
Guests as we know more faithful than *ghosts*

Needless to say, not every problem is so handily solved. For instance, Breton ends his poem "Toutes les écolières ensemble" (All the schoolgirls together) with the lines:

Après une dictée où *Le coeur m'en dit*
S'écrivait peut-être *Le cœur mendie*

Literal translation—"After a dictation where *My heart's desire* /
Might have been written *My heart begs*"—obscures the fact that
m'en dit and *mendie* are pronounced identically, which is especially relevant for a dictation. But we might get a slightly more
evocative (even if still imperfect) idea by rendering these lines a
bit more loosely, as:

> After a dictation where *My heart's urges*
> Might have been written *My heart surges*

"The mind which plunges into Surrealism relives with glow-
ing excitement the best part of its childhood,"[3] Breton wrote,
and much Surrealist wordplay can indeed be traced back to the
verbal games that form part of every schoolchild's inheritance
(which makes you wonder how many ravages will be wrought
on American literature by Dr. Seuss, Edward Gorey, or Maurice
Sendak). Take, for instance, these verbal conundrums, worthy of
Roussel, from which Paul Éluard once fashioned a quatrain: "Les
poules du *couvent couvent*" ("The chickens in the *convent hatch*")
and "Ces dames se *parent* de fleurs pour leur *parent*" ("The ladies
bedeck themselves in flowers for their *relative*"), in which the two
pairs of words, though visually identical, have divergent pronun-
ciations and meanings; or, conversely, the homophonous tour
de force "le *ver* allait *vers* le *verre vert*" ("the *worm* went *toward* the
green glass"). I've yet to see a viable translation of these—but that
doesn't mean it can't be done, by someone with the persistence,
and no doubt the lunacy, to keep at it.

***

More difficult than the conveyance of meaning, and in some
ways even trickier than cultural transposition, sound-based
translation is among the translator's greatest challenges. As any
translator knows, a passage that is heartbreaking, or stirring, or

screamingly funny in the source language can die on arrival, even if the meaning is preserved, simply because the words of the target don't resonate the same way in our inner ear.

To exacerbate the problem, sound has been exploited by certain authors less to give their writing its particular music than to twist language beyond where it normally goes. The novelist Raymond Queneau, in books like *Exercises in Style* and *Zazie in the Metro*, used the sonorities of French in numerous registers, from highest to lowest brow, as an integral part of the plot. Queneau's direct precursor, the nineteenth-century autodidact and outsider author Jean-Pierre Brisset, went so far as to build an entire cosmogony on assonance. In his treatise *The Science of God, or The Creation of Man* (1900), Brisset unveiled several "inescapable" and universal truths based on a chain of homophonous puns, such as the many permutations of the phrase *les dents, la bouche* ("the teeth, the mouth"): *les dents la bouchent* ("the teeth stop it up"), *laides en la bouche* ("ugly in the mouth"), *lait dans la bouche* ("milk in the mouth") …; or his philosophical-scatological variations on sex: "Tu sais que c'est bien. Tu sexe est bien / Je ne sais que c'est. Jeune sexe est" ("You know it's good. You sex is good / I don't know what it is. Young sex is"), and so on. "Everything that is thus written in words and that can be clearly read is imbued with an inescapable truth; it is true the world over," Brisset argued in his personal, and highly Franco-centric, assault on the Tower of Babel. "What is said in one language is said for the entire world. … This is the key to unlock the books of speech."[4]

Whom the gods would destroy they first ridicule: Having self-published several volumes aiming to prove that Man was descended from the Frog, and that French was related (appropriately enough) to frog language, Brisset was named "Prince of

Thinkers" in a bogus election orchestrated by the novelist Jules Romains. He was summoned to Paris and treated to banquets and great ceremony, leaving him overwhelmed by this unexpected show of recognition for his work. Only the next day did he learn from the newspapers that the entire affair was a hoax. Brisset died a few years later, well before his writings sparked the enthusiasm of Queneau, Duchamp, the Surrealists, and Michel Foucault.

A much less grandiose ambition presides over Luis van Rooten's *Mots d'heures: Gousses, rames* (1967), purportedly a transcript of the apocryphal "d'Antin Manuscript," but in fact an extended phonetic joke. Van Rooten, a character actor who specialized in dialects, presented the volume as "curious verses" of uncertain provenance, garlanded with his scholarly apparatus. The first poem, for instance, begins:

> Un petit d'un petit
> S'étonne aux Halles
> Un petit d'un petit
> Ah! degrés te fallent

Literally:

> The son of a small man
> Is stunned at Les Halles [market]
> The son of a small man
> A ladder you need

But just as the "meaning" of one of Monet's Rouen cathedrals is not the edifice itself but the process by which inchoate daubs of paint resolve into the cathedral at different times of day, so the significance of these ditties is revealed not by sight but by reading aloud—at which point we realize that the poem (not unlike Roussel's transformations, or the Zukofskys' homophonic Catullus) is none other than "Humpty Dumpty" as recited by someone with a heavy French accent, and that the entire volume, as the title hints, is really a series of Mother Goose rhymes put through the same process.

Mots d'heures represents a case of perfectly comprehensible, if whimsical, rhymes translated into nonsense. What of the translation of nonsense itself? Arguably the greatest composer of nonsense in the English language was Lewis Carroll, whose writings, despite their linguistic obstacles, have been published in virtually every language in the world. They have made their way multiple times into French, including in a partial version by the Surrealist poet and dramatist Antonin Artaud. (Carroll, not surprisingly, was a favorite of the Surrealists; Louis Aragon translated *The Hunting of the Snark* in 1929.) Artaud, whose own poetry wrenched both the sound and the meaning of French off its hinges, was in some ways the ideal vessel for a French rendition of Carroll, even though he claimed not to like the Englishman's work. Undertaken during his internment at Rodez asylum in the 1940s, and suggested by his psychiatrist as a form of therapy, Artaud's translation of the first stanza of "Jabberwocky" shows just how far down the linguistic rabbit hole he was willing to go. This becomes even clearer by first viewing Carroll's well-known original,

'Twas brillig, and the slithy toves
Did gyre and gimble in the wabe:
All mimsy were the borogoves,
And the mome raths outgrabe.

in this more "standard" French rendering by Henri Parisot:

Il était reveneure; les slictueux toves
Sur l'allouinde gyraient et vriblaient;
Tout flivoreux vaguaient les borogoves;
Les verchons fourgus bourniflaient.

Even without a reading knowledge of French, we can see how Parisot's version stays within the boundaries of Carroll's own permutations, almost as if transcribing rather than translating. Artaud's version, on the other hand, howls from the page in impossible clusters of vowels and consonants that seem to come from nowhere human, including an added intrusion of snarling, otherworldly gibberish in the middle that makes Carroll's already sinister epic even more frightening:

> Il était Roparant, et les vliqueux tarands
> Allaient en gilroyant et en brimbulkdriquant
> Jusque-là où la rourghe est a rouarghe a rangmbde et rangmbde a rouarghambde:
> Tous les falomitards étaient les chats-huants
> Et les Ghoré Uk'hatis dans le GRABÜG-EÛMENT.

Artaud's "Jabberwocky" stands in a free zone between translation and independent work, neither completely original nor, as one scholar has pointed out, liable to be back-translated into anything resembling Carroll's English.[5] In this, it anticipates one of the strangest hybrids of original text and translation ever published, Louis Wolfson's memoir *Le schizo et les langues* (The schizophrenic and languages; 1970). Wolfson, a New Yorker, wrote the book in French (and, for an added measure of distance, in the third person) because he couldn't abide the sound of his mother tongue, literally the tongue of his abhorred mother—a woman who in his telling was loud, grotesque, vulgar, and irredeemably hostile to him. Her very presence acted on his nerves like nails on a chalkboard. Rather than being driven into a frenzy whenever he heard his mother speak—virtually unavoidable, as he lived with her well into adulthood—the self-described "demented student of languages" devised a system in which the offending English sentence would be instantly transposed in his head into a corresponding sentence, patched together from one or more of four foreign languages, which he had taught himself for that purpose. (Perhaps coincidentally, the four languages, French, Hebrew, German, and Russian, are both representative of Wolfson's Eastern European Jewish heritage and virtually the same as those used at Nuremberg.) For the system to work, however, the translated sentence had not only to *mean* but to *sound* the same as the English it replaced. Writes Wolfson about himself:

> He could more or less instantaneously convert another English word into a foreign word, using a method that was certainly bizarre, artificial, and unnatural, but obviously quite acceptable, even necessary, to his poor perverted mind; whereas a simple, accurate, direct translation into a foreign tongue was completely unsatisfactory, since it merely offered his mind a word that was phonetically different from the English word that tortured him, and thus did not procure him the sense of having obliterated that word from his natural language.[6]

As such, Wolfson's "bizarre, artificial, and unnatural" method allowed him to live surrounded by English without mental distress, by convincing himself that what he had really heard was a mishmash—but a *communicative* mishmash—of four non-English languages.

Confronted, for example, with the song "Good Night, Ladies," which his mother frequently plays and sings at top volume on the living-room organ, Wolfson scrambles for a way to keep it from shattering his solipsistic concentration. "The term *ladies* in particular entered involuntarily into the young man's perverted thoughts." After trying out the German *Leute* ("people, folks"), he settles on the Russian *lyudi*, which offers greater phonetic similarity, though it likewise means "people" rather than "women." "The fundamental thing for the schizophrenic student of languages with regard to the similarity between meanings of these

two terms was ... that they both represented the human being,"
Wolfson notes, leaving aside the fact that, in this case especially,
the meaning of the word *ladies* is just as repugnant to him as
its sound. Another episode details how the warning *Don't trip
over the wire!* is painstakingly transmuted over many pages of
trial and error into an amalgam of three languages: *tu'nicht* (German: "do not") *tréb* (French: the start of the verb for "trip") *über*
(German: "over") *èth hé* (from Biblical Hebrew) *zwir[n]* (German:
"thread").

Ultimately, the gratification the young man feels in conquering these English words is proportional to the anxiety they
provoke, each hard-won victory leaving him feeling "much
less miserable than usual, at least for a little while." When, for
instance, the word *where*, the beginning of his mother's frequent
query *Where are my glasses?* finally finds its solution after several
false starts in the German *woher* ("where from"), Wolfson's contentment is profound:

> How pleased he was with himself! What ideas he had! he reflected
> in his naivety, while wondering if anyone else would have thought
> of converting the English *where* into the German *woher*, so that this
> monosyllable would be "scientifically," methodically, immediately,
> totally demolished; of doing it mentally and habitually whenever
> confronted with said monosyllable. ... Even in his mad, not to say
> imbecilic, fashion, how very gratifying it was to study languages!

Le schizo et les langues is a moving, disorienting, at times darkly
hilarious memoir, one that draws the reader deep into Wolfson's
linguistic mania and his tragicomic family dynamic.* It is also

---

* In this, it is reminiscent of Robert Pirsig's probing of philosophy and
madness in *Zen and the Art of Motorcycle Maintenance*. And, as with Pirsig's ultimate acceptance of his delusions, there is desire but also regret
attached to Wolfson's eventual move toward a reconciliation with his
family and with English, a sense of loss.

a remarkable meditation on the act of translation itself—not to mention a brilliant dare to any translator. Sadly, that dare might go forever unanswered, as Wolfson stipulated in his contract with the French publisher that the book should never be translated into English. (Offers to publish it in Italian and German apparently were also rebuffed.)

It's not that Wolfson's language itself resists translation, nor that his minute explorations of interlinguistic phonetics and semantics can't be conveyed in other tongues. These, like the chilly precision and affectlessness of his narrative voice, could be brought over without too much adaptation. Even the irony of reading a book about the abhorrence of English *in English* could be overlooked. My surmise is that the author's stricture against translation has less to do with language than with living. For Wolfson, the sound of English is not merely an annoyance but a deadly threat, a contamination, like the swarms of parasites he imagines around his lips that make him alternate between fasting and bulimia. English is a perpetual attack, a violation. In this all-encompassing system, the mother tongue, as J. M. G. Le Clézio writes, is like "a dangerous infectious area," and each transformed, reconstructed word "an antibody against disease."[7] Wolfson's method, which bears surface similarities to Joyce's and Roussel's but cuts much deeper, takes the notion of linguistic transformation and infuses it with an altogether darker urgency. Upending the traditional criteria of fidelity, style, and authorship, this is philology not as cultural enhancement or aesthetic erudition but as extreme measure, shock therapy, survival.

And as violence. For while the torturing of the already elusive borders between translation, self-translation, and authorship inherent in works such as Wolfson's *Schizo* or Artaud's "Jabberwocky" highlights the nearly inexhaustible malleability of language, it also raises the specter of accountability. If every translation is theoretically possible, how far can we stray from the source before there's no turning back? And if we do stray that far, have we honored the original by creating, in effect, a new original, or have we merely obscured it with our own cleverness (as does, to my mind, Clive Scott's "centrifugal" rendering of Apollinaire's "Annie" in chapter 6)? Harking back to the debate over foreignization, doesn't this risk apply to some degree in any act of translation, forcing us constantly to evaluate, and either sidestep or acquiesce to, acts of personal and cultural violation, as we navigate our way through the text's multiple choices as through a proverbial minefield? Works such as Perec's *La disparition* or Surrealist automatic poetry lay bare some of the more drastic quandaries inherent in the process. But to a greater or lesser extent, in any project undertaken, the translator is always dancing on the fringe.

9 Adam's Apricot, or Does Translation Matter?

Sometime in the mid-1600s, the blind poet and political activist John Milton deployed one of the most influential mistranslations in the history of literature. Leaning on biblical tradition, he began his epic *Paradise Lost* by invoking "the Fruit / Of that Forbidden Tree, whose mortal tast / Brought Death into the World." In this, Milton was following centuries of scholarship, which usually translates the Hebrew term *peri* as a generic "fruit," sometimes likening it to a fig, citron, apricot, or pomegranate (Michelangelo's man-serpent on the Sistine ceiling, for instance, hugs a fig tree). But some seven thousand lines later, Milton returned to the scene of the crime to ID his forbidden fruit in a way that's been familiar to us ever since: "To satisfie the sharp desire I had / Of tasting those fair Apples, I resolv'd / Not to deferr ..." Was this pure fancy? Perhaps, but not on Milton's part. Like most learned Christians of his time, Milton took his cues largely from Saint Jerome's Vulgate, and it was Jerome who, coming upon the forbidden timber in his Hebrew source text, had created a Latin pun, essentially turning the Tree of the Knowledge of Good and Evil (*malum*) into the tree of apples (*malus*).

Or something along those lines, for even *malus* could, in Jerome's day, mean not only "apple" but any number of other fleshy fruits, such as pears or peaches. Enter Albrecht Dürer, whose engraving *Adam and Eve* (1504) shows the couple beside an unmistakable apple tree, made still more unmistakable in his painted version of 1507, and again in Lucas Cranach the Elder's painting of the same scene from around 1530. And even then, Milton, over a century later, might himself have been using *apple* in a more generic sense—Eve's intoxication after partaking of the Forbidden Fruit is more suggestive of grapes—but somewhere along the line, his "fair Apples" came to mean the bright rubine *Malus pumila* that we know today.[1] In other words, from Hebrew to Latin to English, by way of German visual arts, an essential trope of our cultural and religious mythology was founded on what amounts to a mistranslation, or at least a misreading.

One could object that regardless of whether Eve bit into a forbidden apple or pomegranate, the transgressive substance of the message remains the same, and that the course of humanity probably would not have altered if we instead referred to the eponymous bit of neck cartilage as an "Adam's apricot." Then again, who's to say exactly what impact the fruit of Original Sin has had in the last two millennia (or at least in the centuries since Milton) precisely because it was an apple? Symbols are powerful things, and this one in particular is of enough universal notoriety to suggest that the apple is not just an apple, even if we can't decide whether it's also a citron or a fig.

Other mistranslations, meanwhile, have had more easily demonstrable consequences. Jerome, again, in his description of Moses's head as he descends from Mount Sinai (Exodus 34:29), mistook the Hebrew word *karan*, or "radiance," for *keren*, meaning "horned"—a potentially humorous slip that any editor might have queried. Nonetheless, from it originated the protuberances on Moses's forehead in Michelangelo's sculpture in the church of San Pietro in Vincoli and, much less humorously, the longstanding anti-Semitic stereotype of Jews as sprouting devilish horns. And another religious misapprehension that could and should have been avoided: the phrase *Satanic verses*, referring to one or several suppressed verses in the Quran (which the Prophet Muhammad is said to have repudiated as having been suggested by Satan), is actually not used in the Muslim world. It is an invention of nineteenth-century British Orientalists, whereas in Arabic, these rejected lines are referred to as *gharaniq*, meaning "the cranes." When Salman Rushdie's novel *The Satanic Verses* was published in Arabic, the translator rendered the title literally but in the event incorrectly, thereby inadvertently suggesting, not the excised "crane" verses, but rather that the Quran itself had been dictated by Satan. The perceived blasphemy, unintended by the author, led to international rioting, the *fatwa* against Rushdie, his enforced seclusion and the breakup of his marriage, the murder of the book's Japanese translator, Hitoshi Igarashi, and the attempted murder of its Italian translator, Ettore Capriolo.[2]

***

Does translation matter? Various misrepresentations throughout history, such as Nikita Khrushchev's over-translated "We will bury you" and the Cold War paranoia it fueled (the Russian phrase was actually a prematurely boastful "We will outlast you"), have shown how much can turn on a single word. Empires have been won and lost, crucial actions taken or neglected, on the strength of how a translator did or didn't convey certain information. The events of September 11, 2001, and the tragic aftereffects they have had on lives and national attitudes, might have been averted had the messages in Arabic intercepted on September 10 been processed sooner than the twelfth.[3] Sometimes it's as subtle as a difference in nuance: when in July 1945 the Allies issued an ultimatum for Japan's unconditional surrender, Premier Suzuki's response to reporters' pressing questions was, "No comment. We need more time." But Suzuki used the word *mokusatsu*, which can also mean, in effect, "Yeah, yeah, whatever," and that is how it got back to Harry Truman. Ten days later, "Little Boy" decimated Hiroshima.

These are only some of the better-known instances. They, and thousands of others like them throughout history, give haunting proof of the impact that interlingual communication, and its all-too-frequent breakdown, can have. And as the global reach of nations grows more pronounced, their weapons more destructive, their business dealings more intertwined, the need for reliable forms of cross-cultural understanding becomes all the more urgent—not only in the realm of statecraft, but also in the everyday spheres of medicine, commerce, research, communications, entertainment, and so on.

But there's another way to frame the question, one that has less to do with geopolitics and more with cultural amplitude. Earlier, I contested the frequently voiced notion that publishing and consuming literary translations is some kind of ethical imperative. This view, held by many translators as well as by organizations like PEN International and Words without Borders, is articulated by Edith Grossman like this:

> Translation not only plays an important traditional role as the means that allows us access to literature originally written in one of the countless languages we cannot read, but it also represents a concrete literary presence with the crucial capacity to ease and make more meaningful our relationships to those with whom we may not have had a connection before. Translation always helps us to know, to see from a different angle, to attribute new value to what once may have been unfamiliar.[4]

Translation, in other words, is what opens the path, and keeps it open, to the world of attitudes, viewpoints, and modes of expression beyond our local parameters. It is what keeps us receptive to possibilities other than those suggested by our own linguistic and cultural experience. Eliot Weinberger reminds us that "cultures that do not translate stagnate, and end up repeating the same things to themselves." Or, in George Steiner's motivating and chilling dictum, without translators "we would live in arrogant parishes bordered by silence."[5] Translation takes the fact that cultures are by nature amalgamations of other cultures and pushes it to the head of the class. It keeps us aware of the uncontrollably heteroclite subsoil beneath any cultural surface, however undifferentiated that surface might appear.

One common cliché is that if there were only one language in the world, or if by some miracle humans could read and understand all languages, the need for translation would evaporate. It's true that, were we to take language strictly as a conveyer of facts simple and straight, then perhaps translation would become superfluous in a world where everyone immediately grasped what everyone else was saying. Translation, however, fills a function beyond mere data transmission, which is why talking about "equivalences" is so pointless. Instead, as a mediator and re-creator, translation provides a new way of looking at a text, and through that text a world, as represented by someone with an entirely distinct (though presumably complementary) vision. And, as I've stressed many times in this book, it allows for the emergence of a new literary work, at once dependent on and independent of the work that prompted it.

This is where I can't help but feel uneasy with the moral subtext of statements such as Grossman's, however much I agree with them in spirit. On the one hand, I recognize the ethical benefit of seeing things from different angles, breaking out of our arrogant parishes. At the same time, there is a true-believer aspect to this way of putting the matter that ultimately does translation a disservice—not helped by the fact that the listings for many presses, especially the earnest independents, tend to skew toward a fairly homogenous, equally earnest, profile. As with many well-meaning efforts, the accent is laid on *should*s and *ought*s, whereas the real joy of translation is precisely the new vistas it affords, the thrill of discoveries not otherwise possible, the appeal to our sense of pleasure rather than duty. I prefer to consider translation a fine liqueur, not a medicine. But too often it comes bottled with a prescriptive label.

That said, translation in this more joyful sense depends on a world situation that might itself be disappearing. When I think of translation, I think not so much of bridges as of borders, their dissolution but also their utility. In our increasingly interconnected world, it is not only tempting but logical to posit the end of national and cultural boundaries. It's a position held by many, and one that to a large extent I endorse, especially since, as I write this, border-related issues are the excuse for many of the abuses perpetrated by the world's governments, mine included. Politicians rail about the dangers of unchecked migration, of infiltration by the villains du jour; but these threats have existed, in one form or other, since before the time of Troy, and never has the intensification of borders substantially changed that fact, or the benefits regimes have derived from them.

What concerns and puzzles me more is the infiltration of homogeneity, for borders can also be seen as guardians of difference. The flip side of unrestricted circulation, as well as of potentially infinite contact (including, paradoxically, the kind of contact made possible by translation), is that it can also lead to the erosion of diversity. What concerns me is the emergence of a world in which translation really is no longer necessary, not because we can all speak the same language but because the world's languages no longer express the psychological and cultural differences that make them distinct and interesting. Earlier, I characterized translation as both the bridge linking cultures and a measure of the distance between them. But what happens when that distance becomes negligible? What happens when you can go anywhere in the world and find the same McD's, the same Starbucks, the same Gap, the same Apple Store, and—most insidious of all—the same basic outlook, regardless of whether you're in Paris, Prague, or Parsippany? What would be the point of traveling under such conditions, whether physically or in the pages of a foreign novel?

In this regard, the defiant catchphrase "Art has no borders" becomes both an aspiration and a threat. The diffusion of ideas, the intellectual and aesthetic free-for-all of arts, literatures, philosophies, and viewpoints ricocheting throughout the world, aided and abetted by our ever-faster messaging media, could bring one of the greatest revitalizations of cultures in the history of humankind, a new Renaissance. Or it could lead to the blandest global monoculture we've ever known. I would argue that, in significant measure, this will depend on how the translation of these ideas is handled, and whether it can maintain its freedom. In this regard, it is crucial not to let translation be co-opted by commercial interests (obscuring the fact that it *is* a translation, for instance, or choosing only those foreign texts that reinforce the domestic conversation), by political strictures (of whichever wing), by moral injunctions ("Read this, it's good for you"), or by academic vogue. It is necessary to claim for translation the same rights, responsibilities, prerogatives, and pleasures that we accord any form of artistic expression—first and foremost, the right to speak with authority and invention.*

And, while we're at it, let's be sure to leave a creative space for mistranslation. Misinterpretation can lead to disastrous treaty negotiations or religious upheavals, but it can also give us Eve's apple. We know that writers throughout history have influenced later writers in other languages (such as Faulkner's influence on the Latin American Boom, which in return energized a subsequent generation of US authors; or the inspiration that modern Chinese poets took from Pound's *Cathay*), and of course this ping-pong of influences has most often taken place via translation. But the more interesting question is, how many essential works can be traced to an unwittingly fruitful misinterpretation, whether on the reader's part or the translator's? It's perhaps an impossible question to answer, but Adam Thirlwell, in *The Delighted States*, gives us a hint when he posits that erroneous translations can sometimes be more seminal, literarily speaking, than accurate ones. Specifically, Thirlwell brings up the Russian Pushkin and the Brazilian Machado de Assis, both taking inspiration from poor French translations of Laurence Sterne's *Tristram Shandy* and *A Sentimental Journey*. "My baffled conclusion is that the version of Sterne they were reading was an entirely plausible one; it was still useful. … It is obvious that in Rio de Janeiro, or St. Petersburg, reading this approximation to a rough translation, it was still possible to see what Sterne was up to and develop his techniques." And Thirlwell concludes

---

* To clarify for those who feel I've just contradicted what I said in chapter 6 about Clive Scott's Apollinaire: I defend his right to be as fanciful as he likes, just as I defend mine to find his exercise inane. That said, should it someday inspire someone to create a new and brilliant piece of writing, more power to it.

with an aphorism that applies equally well to translation: "Every theory of literature has to incorporate a theory of the fluke."[6]

***

In the end, the importance of translation might just be to safeguard those distances it supposedly is meant to bridge. I'm not talking about keeping cultures apart, of course, but about helping ensure that the contact produces sparks rather than suffocation. At the same time, the point is not, as proponents of foreignization would have it, to make funny-sounding translations that ape another language's syntax but rather to bring in foreign viewpoints; and not to sanitize these viewpoints in the interests of the target audience but to preserve the source author's thought and expression in a target idiom that speaks to that audience, even while conveying something radically unlike anything it has conveyed before. As I mentioned earlier, the single most valuable service translation can render is to identify and bring us into contact with those rare minds and voices that are truly unique, that have something to say that is dissimilar from what anyone else has to say. That make a difference, in every sense of the word. That literally change our minds.

Somewhere beyond our linguistic, cultural, and attitudinal borders, a thought or viewpoint born of a context distinct from ours is being formed, will be expressed, and will have the power to move the world, or at least our world. The best we can hope for is to find it before everything becomes so hopelessly alike that no such expression can be conceived—because once that happens, translation, and the ancient impetus that fostered it, really will cease to matter.

Notes

Introduction

1. Johann Wolfgang von Goethe, letter of July 20, 1827, *Correspondence Between Goethe and Carlyle*, ed. Charles Eliot Norton (London: Macmillan, 1887), 26.

2. Gregory Rabassa, *If This Be Treason: Translation and Its Dyscontents* (New York: New Directions, 2006), 8.

Chapter 1

1. David Bellos has noted that in Japan, certain translators are famous enough to have entire series of books devoted to their work, their name on the cover as large as the author's. For instance, Haruki Murakami is known not only as the best-selling novelist familiar to Western readers, but also as the celebrated translator of authors like Truman Capote, Raymond Carver, F. Scott Fitzgerald, and J. D. Salinger. See David Bellos, *Is That a Fish in Your Ear? Translation and the Meaning of Everything* (New York: Faber and Faber, 2011; hereafter "Bellos"), 292. See also Haruki Murakami, "As Translator, as Novelist: The Translator's Afterword," in *In Translation: Translators on Their Work and What It Means*, ed. Esther Allen and Susan Bernofsky (New York: Columbia University Press, 2013), 169–182.

2. Alice Kaplan, "Translation: The Biography of an Artform," in Allen and Bernofsky, *In Translation*, 79.

3. Horace, *Ars poetica* (The art of poetry), trans. H. Rushton Fairclough, in *Translation—Theory and Practice: A Historical Reader*, ed. Daniel Weissbort and Astradur Eysteinsson (New York: Oxford University Press, 2006; hereafter "*TTP*"), 22; John Denham, "To Sir Richard Fanshaw upon his Translation of [Giovanni Battista Guarini's] Pastor Fido," ibid., 121; Cicero, *De optimo genere oratorum* (On the best kind of orator), trans. L. G. Kelly, ibid., 21; Boethius, introduction to his commentary on Porphyry's *Isagoge*, trans. L. G. Kelly, ibid., 33.

Most of the texts collected in *TTP* are from previously published sources; for all quotations from those texts in this book, see *TTP* for full source citation.

4. For a far more nuanced discussion of this mutually beneficial adaptation, see Denis Feeney, *Beyond Greek: The Beginnings of Latin Literature* (Cambridge, MA: Harvard University Press, 2016).

5. Umberto Eco, *Experiences in Translation*, trans. Alastair McEwen (Toronto: University of Toronto Press, 2001), ix.

6. José Ortega y Gasset, "The Misery and the Splendor of Translation," in *Theories of Translation: An Anthology of Essays from Dryden to Derrida*, ed. Rainer Schulte and John Biguenet (Chicago: University of Chicago Press, 1992), 93; Paul Ricoeur, *On Translation*, trans. Eileen Brennan (London: Routledge, 2006), 8.

7. George Steiner, *After Babel: Aspects of Language and Translation* (New York: Oxford University Press, 1975), 172; see especially the chapters "Language and Gnosis" and "The Claims of Theory."

8. Bellos, 84–85.

9. Ricoeur, *On Translation*, 5.

10. Susan Bassnett, *Translation* (London: Routledge, 2014), 150 and 11 (see also 158–159); Bassnett, *Translation Studies*, rev. ed. (London: Routledge, 1991), 55; John Dryden, "On Translation" (preface to Ovid's *Epistles*), in Schulte and Biguenet, *Theories of Translation*, 22.

11. Suzanne Jill Levine, *The Subversive Scribe: Translating Latin American Fiction* (Saint Paul, MN: Graywolf, 1991), 19.

12. Peter Cole, "Making Sense in Translation: Toward an Ethics of the Art," in Allen and Bernofsky, *In Translation*, 5.

13. Jorge Luis Borges, quoted by Levine, *Subversive Scribe*, 1; Umberto Eco, *Mouse or Rat?: Translation as Negotiation*, quoted in *The Translator as Writer*, ed. Susan Bassnett and Peter Bush (New York: Continuum, 2006), 60 (cf. Eco, *Experiences*, 7–8); Maurice Blanchot, "Translating," trans. Richard Sieburth, *Sulfur* 26 (1990), 82; Edmund Keeley, "Collaboration, Revision, and Other Less Forgivable Sins in Translation," in *The Craft of Translation*, ed. John Biguenet and Rainer Schulte (Chicago: University of Chicago Press, 1989), 57.

14. Milan Kundera, *Testaments Betrayed: An Essay in Nine Parts* (New York: HarperPerennial, 1996), 110, 108.

15. See, for instance, Robert McCrum, William Cran, and Robert Mac-Neil, *The Story of English* (New York: Penguin, 1992), 10; "Number of Words in the English Language," in *The Physics Factbook*, accessed April 17, 2017, http://hypertextbook.com/facts/2001/JohnnyLing.shtml.

16. Kundera, *Testaments*, 109.

17. Murakami, "As Translator, as Novelist," 173.

Chapter 2

1. Eliot Weinberger, "Anonymous Sources (On Translators and Translation)," in Allen and Bernofsky, *In Translation*, 22–23, 49; Eco, *Experiences*, 74; Michael Hanne, "Metaphors for the Translator," in Bassnett and Bush, *Translator as Writer*, 208, 214. For a contrarian view of the "bearing across" metaphor as detrimental to a true understanding of translation, see Bellos, 33ff. According to Steiner (*After Babel*, 295), the Romance language derivation was itself based on a mistranslation, as *traducere* actually means "to introduce" or "to lead into"—a "trivial but symbolic" difference, he writes.

2. Bassnett, *Translation Studies*, 15. Koiné, or "the common dialect," also known as "Biblical" or "New Testament" Greek, is still used today in the liturgies of the Greek Orthodox Church.

3. Jerome, preface to the *Chronicles* of Eusebius 1–2, trans. L. G. Kelly, in *TTP*, 29. See also Bassnett, *Translation Studies*, 46–48; Eugene A. Nida, *Toward a Science of Translating* (Leiden: E. J. Brill, 1964), 12; Theodore H. Savory, *The Art of Translation* (London: Jonathan Cape, 1957), 104–107; Nataly Kelly and Jost Zetzsche, *Found in Translation: How Language Shapes Our Lives and Transforms the World* (New York: Perigee, 2012), 121–122; *TTP*, 68–69; Bassnett, *Translation*, 10.

4. Augustine, Letter 71.3–4 and 6, trans. L. G. Kelly, in *TTP*, 32.

5. Martin Luther, *Open Letter on Translation*, trans. Jennifer Tanner, in *TTP*, 57; Johann Wolfgang von Goethe, *Dichtung und Wahrheit*, trans. André Lefevere, in *TTP*, 200.

6. William Tyndale, "W.T. to the Reader" (preface to Tyndale's translation of Genesis), in *TTP*, 69.

7. Savory, *Art of Translation*, 107. Quotes on Bible translation from *TTP*, 200, 264, 69, 116, and Nida, *Toward a Science*, 17. George Steiner (*After Babel*, 348) notes that the King James translators achieved this "unequalled feeling of 'at-homeness' ... a new pivot of English self-consciousness" by adopting a form of expression that pre-dated them by two or three generations.

8. Everett Fox, translator's preface and Genesis 2:1–9, in *TTP*, 562–563, 568.

9. Nida, *Toward a Science*, 156, 158, 168; Nida, "Principles of Translation as Exemplified by Bible Translating," in *On Translation*, ed. Reuben A. Brower (Cambridge, MA: Harvard University Press, 1959), 12, 19. See also Bellos, 170–171.

10. *La Bible: Nouvelle traduction* (Montrouge: Bayard, 2015), 22.

11. Bassnett, *Translation*, 90.

12. See Corrado Federici, review of Charles Le Blanc's French translation of *De interpretatione recta, TTR: Traduction, Terminologie, Rédaction* 23, no. 1 (2010): 191–194, accessed January 16, 2017, http://id.erudit.org/iderudit/044934ar.

13. Étienne Dolet, *La manière de bien traduire d'une langue en aultre*, trans. James S. Holmes, in *TTP*, 73–76.

14. Thomas Wilson, preface to *The Three Orations of Demosthenes*, in *TTP*, 89. See also ibid., 211; Bassnett, *Translation*, 76.

15. Kenneth Rexroth, "The Poet as Translator," in *World Outside the Window: The Selected Essays of Kenneth Rexroth*, ed. Bradford Morrow (New York: New Directions, 1987), 171; Dryden, preface to Ovid's *Epistles*, 18, 31.

16. Alexander Fraser Tytler, *Essay on the Principles of Translation*, in *TTP*, 190, 193.

17. R. H. Horne, "Remarks on Translation," ibid., 213.

18. George Eliot, "Translations and Translators," ibid., 220.

19. F. W. Newman, preface to *The Iliad of Homer*, ibid., 226; Matthew Arnold, *On Translating Homer*, ibid., 227, 229–230. See also Bassnett, *Translation Studies*, 69.

20. Richard Bentley, quoted in *TTP*, 166; Dante Gabriel Rossetti, preface to *The Early Italian Poets*, ibid., 254. Pound's retort to Bentley: "[Pope] has at least the merit of translating Homer into *something*."

21. Lt. Col. Paul T. Darling, " 'Terps to Troops," *Armed Forces Journal*, February 1, 2011, accessed January 8, 2017, http://armedforcesjournal.com/terps-to-troops; cf. Kelly and Zetzsche, *Found in Translation*, 39.

22. Jean Findlay, *Chasing Lost Time: The Life of C. K. Scott Moncrieff, Soldier, Spy, and Translator* (New York: Farrar, Straus, and Giroux, 2015), 3–4, 210, 215–217, 227–229.

23. Bernard Turle, *Diplomat, Actor, Translator, Spy*, Cahier 19 (Paris: Center for Writers and Translators, American University of Paris, 2013), 12.

Chapter 3

1. Friedrich Schleiermacher, "On the Different Methods of Translating," trans. André Lefevere, in *TTP*, 207–208; Goethe, quoted by Lawrence Venuti, *The Scandals of Translation: Towards an Ethics of Difference* (London: Routledge, 1998), 77.

2. Schleiermacher, "Different Methods," 209. Cf. Lawrence Venuti, *The Translator's Invisibility: A History of Translation* (London: Routledge, 1995), 117–118. In a similar vein, about fifty years earlier, the German philosopher and critic Johann Gottfried Herder had likened translation to walking "through foreign gardens to pick flowers for my language."

3. Quotes in this and the following three paragraphs: Walter Benjamin, "The Task of the Translator," in *Illuminations*, trans. Harry Zohn (New York: Schocken, 1969), 69, 70, 71, 74, 75, 76–77, 78–80. Cf. Steiner, *After Babel*, 300: "The work translated is enhanced. … To class a source-text as worth translating is to dignify it immediately and to involve it in a dynamic of magnification."

4. André Breton, "Second Manifesto of Surrealism," in *Manifestoes of Surrealism*, trans. Richard Seaver and Helen R. Lane (Ann Arbor: University of Michigan Press, 1969), 123.

5. André Lefevere, "German Translation Theory: Legacy and Relevance," quoted by Venuti, *Translator's Invisibility*, 117 (see also 318); Astradur Eysteinsson and Daniel Weissbort, introduction to *TTP*, 4 (citing title of talk by James S. Holmes); James S. Holmes, "Describing Literary Translations: Models and Methods," in *TTP*, 421. The "underdeveloped country" has now become quite developed, some might even say overdeveloped; for a good cross section of current theory, see *The Translation Studies Reader*, ed. Lawrence Venuti (London: Routledge, 2004).

6. Kenneth Goldsmith, *Against Translation: Displacement Is the New Translation* (Paris: Jean Boîte, 2014), 1, 3, 4–5; John Cage, foreword to *M: Writings '67–'72*, quoted ibid.

7. See also Joshua Foer's article about a man losing control of his own invented language: "Utopian for Beginners," *New Yorker*, December 24/31, 2012, 86–97.

8. Warren Weaver, "Translation," quoted by Sergei Nirenburg, Jaime Carbonell, Masaru Tomita, and Kenneth Goodman, *Machine Translation: A Knowledge-Based Approach* (San Mateo, CA: Morgan Kaufmann, 1992), 3. Ludwig Wittgenstein had slightly anticipated this when he wrote, "Translating from one language into another is a mathematical task, and the translation of a lyrical poem, for example, into a foreign language is quite analogous to a mathematical *problem*" (Ludwig Wittgenstein, *Zettel*, 698, quoted by Steiner, *After Babel*, 275).

9. Bellos, 247–258, 260; Nirenburg et al., *Machine Translation*, 2–7. For additional examples, see ibid., 11, and Nida, *Toward a Science*, 262.

10. Nirenburg et al., *Machine Translation*, 9–10.

11. Anthony G. Oettinger, "Automatic (Transference, Translation, Remittance, Shunting)," in Brower, *On Translation*, 258. More recently, the chief executive of the Russian company ProMT, which makes MT software for corporate clients, speculated that one could use their program to produce a rough draft of a literary translation, although "someone should fine-tune it before publishing" (*Publishers Weekly*, April 20, 2009, 16). The iPhone app Babelshot similarly claims to "work great with foreign newspapers, booklets, menus, even product manuals," but leaves the classics of world literature out of it. For his part, the inventor Ray Kurzweil predicts that machines will reach human levels of understanding of language by 2029 (Kelly and Zetzsche, *Found in Translation*, 230).

12. For a case study of how well Google fares with literature, see Esther Allen, "Can Google Help Translate a Classic Novel?" *Publishers Weekly*, August 26, 2016, accessed October 22, 2017, https://www.publishersweekly.com/pw/by-topic/industry-news/tip-sheet/article/71273-google-translating-a-classic-novel.html.

13. Kelly and Zetzsche, *Found in Translation*, 226.

Chapter 4

1. John Dryden, "Dedication to the *Aeneis*," in *TTP*, 150; Hanne, "Metaphors," 218; Edith Grossman, *Why Translation Matters* (New Haven, CT: Yale University Press, 2010; hereafter "Grossman"), 67; Eco, *Experiences*, 8; Borges, quoted by Grossman, 72–73.

2. Mark Twain, *The Jumping Frog: In English, Then in French, and Then Clawed Back Into A Civilized Language Once More by Patient, Unremunerated Toil*, quoted by Bellos, 107. See also 102–116 for a discussion of the "myth of literal translation."

3. Lawrence Venuti, "Local Contingencies: Translation and National Identities," in *Nation, Language, and the Ethics of Translation*, ed. Sandra Bermann and Michael Wood (Princeton, NJ: Princeton University Press, 2005), 182.

4. Vladimir Nabokov, "The Art of Translation, I: A Few Perfect Rules," in *Verses and Versions: Three Centuries of Russian Poetry*, ed. Brian Boyd and Stanislav Shvabrin (New York: Harcourt, 2008), 4; Judson Rosengrant, letter to the editor, *New York Review of Books*, September 29, 2016, 93; Cole, "Making Sense," 23, 25; Rabassa's retort has been widely reproduced.

5. Constance Garnett, "The Art of Translation," in *TTP*, 292. See also Bassnett, *Translation*, 68, 78; Bassnett, *Translation Studies*, 59.

6. Burton Raffel, "Translating Medieval European Poetry," in Biguenet and Schulte, *Craft of Translation*, 35.

7. Saint Jerome, letter to Pammachius "On the Best Method of Translating," quoted by Hugo Friedrich, "On the Art of Translation," in Schulte and Biguenet, *Theories of Translation*, 12–13. An alternate version reads: "Like a conqueror he has led away captive into his own tongue the meaning of his originals."

8. Susan Sontag, "The World as India: The St. Jerome Lecture on Literary Translation," in *At the Same Time: Essays and Speeches* (New York: Farrar, Straus, and Giroux, 2007), 177.

9. Emily Apter, *The Translation Zone: A New Comparative Literature* (Princeton, NJ: Princeton University Press, 2006), 4. According to Kelly and Zetzsche, the internet might be reversing the erasure of minor languages (*Found in Translation*, 24).

10. Sandra Bermann, introduction to Bermann and Wood, *Nation, Language, Ethics*, 1.

11. Cole, "Making Sense," 10.

12. Quotes in this and the following paragraph from Venuti, *Translator's Invisibility*, 78, 18, 20, 1.

13. Bellos, 58. See also 36.

14. Grossman, 10–11.

15. Alexander Fraser Tytler, *Essay on the Principles of Translation*, quoted by Venuti, *Translator's Invisibility*, 69–72; J. H. Frere, review of T. Mitchell's translations of Aristophanes (1820), quoted ibid., 80.

16. Edward FitzGerald, letter to E. B. Cowell, in *TTP*, 241.

17. FitzGerald, letter to James Russell Lowell, ibid., 246. Cf. Bassnett, *Translation*, 94–95.

18. Venuti, *Translator's Invisibility*, 18.

19. John Balcom, "Translating Modern Chinese Literature," in Bassnett and Bush, *Translator as Writer*, 119.

20. Borges, quoted by Weinberger, "Anonymous Sources," 27.

21. Truda Spruyt, "Translated Fiction at Its Finest," *Publishers Weekly: Frankfurt Show Daily*, October 15, 2015, 41–42; John Maher, "NBF to Conduct Translation Study," *Publishers Weekly*, October 4, 2016, accessed May 8, 2017, https://www.publishersweekly.com/pw/by-topic/industry-news/bookselling/article/71659-nbf-to-conduct-translation-study.html; "Amazon Launches Translation Imprint, AmazonCrossing," *Publishers Weekly*, May 19, 2010, accessed May 8, 2017, https://www.publishersweekly.com/pw/by-topic/industry-news/publisher-news/article/43225-amazon-launches-translation-imprint-amazoncrossing

.html; Chad W. Post, "By the Numbers—A Surge in Translations," *Publishers Weekly: Frankfurt Show Daily*, October 20, 2016, 18–19. As reported by Post, between 2010, when the imprint started, and 2016, Amazon-Crossing published 237 original translations; the next highest output during that period was from Dalkey Archive, with 192 titles. See also Grossman, 28.

22. See Bill Morris, "Why Americans Don't Read Foreign Fiction," *The Daily Beast*, February 4, 2015, accessed August 4, 2017, http://www.thedailybeast.com/why-americans-dont-read-foreign-fiction.

23. Venuti, *Translator's Invisibility*, 20. See also his remarks about the poor standing of translations in academia: Venuti, *Scandals*, 1.

24. Tim Parks, "The Expendable Translator," *New York Review of Books*, March 28, 2017, accessed August 26, 2017, http://www.nybooks.com/daily/2017/03/28/the-expendable-translator/.

25. Bermann, introduction to Bermann and Wood, *Nation, Language, Ethics*, 7; Grossman, 59; Andre Dubus III, introduction to *Words Without Borders: The World Through the Eyes of Writers*, quoted by Grossman, 52.

Chapter 5

1. Laura Bohannan, "Shakespeare in the Bush," in *TTP*, 371–375.

2. Noam Chomsky, in the documentary *We Still Live Here*, quoted by Kelly and Zetzsche, *Found in Translation*, 29; Rabassa, *If This Be Treason*, 7; Richard Lourie and Aleksei Mikhailov, "Why You'll Never Have Fun in Russian," quoted by Lynn Visson, "Simultaneous Interpretation: Language and Cultural Difference," in Bermann and Wood, *Nation, Language, Ethics*, 57–58.

3. Tim Parks, *Translating Style*, 2nd ed. (London: Routledge, 2014), 243.

4. Lawrence Venuti, "Translation, Community, Utopia," in Venuti, *Translation Studies Reader*, 497. Cf. Mark Polizzotti, "Change of Plans: *Plan of Occupancy* Revisited," *Columbia Journal* 54 (spring 2016): 129–139. For a recent translation of Patrick Modiano, a similarly economical

craftsman, I did a comparative word count of the English and French, then combed through my version to eliminate any unnecessary words, bringing my translation more in tune with the sparseness of Modiano's prose—even when it meant reordering syntax, or finding one English word to stand in for several in French. Can such alterations truly yield a better fit to the "beautiful body" of the original? Yes, I believe they can.

5. Kelly and Zetzsche, *Found in Translation*, 176–178.

6. Shoshana Blum-Kulka, "Shifts of Cohesion and Coherence in Translation," in Venuti, *Translation Studies Reader*, 297; Kelly and Zetzsche, *Found in Translation*, 75.

7. Richard Howard, "A Professional Translator's Trade Alphabet," in *The Craft and Context of Translation*, ed. William Arrowsmith and Roger Shattuck (Austin: University of Texas Press, 1961), 166; Bellos, 169.

8. Marcel Rioux, *Les Québécois*, quoted by Annie Brisset, "The Search for a Native Language: Translation and Cultural Identity," in Venuti, *Translation Studies Reader*, 342. See also 343, 358–359, 361.

9. Quoted by Visson, "Simultaneous Interpretation," 58.

10. "Crucial and elusive": Esther Allen, "The Will to Translate: Four Episodes in a Local History of Global Cultural Exchange," in Allen and Bernofsky, *In Translation*, 95; "Dickensianity" and so on: Bellos, 289–290.

11. Adam Thirlwell, *The Delighted States* (New York: Picador, 2010), 89; Doris Lessing, interview in *Premio Mondello: Letteratura 1975–1987*, quoted by Parks, *Translating Style*, 241.

12. Marcel Proust, *Contre Sainte-Beuve*, quoted ibid., 240.

13. Robert Douglas-Fairhurst, "In Search of Marcel Proust," quoted by Findlay, *Chasing Lost Time*, 298 (see also 195, 197, 297, 216–217); Lydia Davis, "Some Notes on Translation and on Madame Bovary," *The Paris Review* 198 (fall 2011), accessed August 21, 2017, https://www .theparisreview.org/letters-essays/6109/some-notes-on-translation-and -on-madame-bovary-lydia-davis; D. H. Lawrence, foreword to *Women in Love*, quoted by Parks, *Translating Style*, 15.

14. Dryden, "Dedication to the *Aeneis*," 150; Benjamin, "Task of the Translator," 73.

15. Jorge Luis Borges, "Pierre Menard, Author of Don Quixote," trans. Anthony Bonner, in *Ficciones*, ed. Anthony Kerrigan (New York: Grove, 1962), 52–53.

16. Edwin Muir and Willa Muir, "Translating from the German," in Brower, *On Translation*, 93.

17. Ryan Bloom, "Lost in Translation: What the First Line of 'The Stranger' Should Be," *New Yorker*, May 11, 2012, accessed May 28, 2017, http://www.newyorker.com/books/page-turner/lost-in-translation -what-the-first-line-of-the-stranger-should-be.

18. Ralph Manheim, trans., *Journey to the End of the Night*, by Louis-Ferdinand Céline (New York: New Directions, 2006), 16. The sentence translates more colloquially as: "Let's hope they've bumped him off by now (and I don't mean easy-peasy)." In a 1957 essay titled "L'argot est né de la haine," Céline posited that "Hate gave birth to slang. Slang is for expressing how deprivation really feels."

19. All quotes from Breon Mitchell, translator's afterword to Gunter Grass, *The Tin Drum* (New York: Houghton Mifflin Harcourt, 2009), 569–570.

20. Eco, *Experiences*, 115; Michael Wood, "Power of Babble," *Bookforum*, summer 2008, 26.

21. Venuti, *Scandals*, 6. Cf. Bassnett, *Translation*, 49–50.

22. Susan Bernofsky, "Translation and the Art of Revision," in Allen and Bernofsky, *In Translation*, 233; Frank O. Copley, translation of Catullus, Poem 13, quoted by Bassnett, *Translation Studies*, 85; Celia and Louis Zukofsky, *Catullus*, quoted by Venuti, *Translator's Invisibility*, 215 (the "normal" English line is by Charles Martin, *The Poems of Catullus*, quoted ibid.).

23. Rabassa, *If This Be Treason*, 8; Matthew Reynolds, *The Poetry of Translation*, quoted by Bassnett, *Translation*, 152.

Chapter 6

1. Leonora Carrington, quoted by Parul Sehgal, "The Romance and Heartbreak of Writing in a Language Not Your Own," *New York Times*, June 4, 2017, BR59.

2. Rabassa, *If This Be Treason*, 63.

3. Ibid., 97–98.

4. William Weaver, "The Process of Translation," in Biguenet and Schulte, *Craft of Translation*, 117. For a discussion of the joys of translating, see Lydia Davis, "Eleven Pleasures of Translating," *New York Review of Books*, December 8, 2016, accessed August 4, 2017, http://www.nybooks.com/articles/2016/12/08/eleven-pleasures-of-translating/, and Davis, "Some Notes on Translation."

5. Weinberger, "Anonymous Sources," 28; John Rutherford, "Translating Fun: *Don Quixote*," in Bassnett and Bush, *Translator as Writer*, 79; Bellos, 199.

6. Weaver, "Process of Translation," 117.

7. Ricoeur, *On Translation*, 22.

8. André Gide, quoted by Justin O'Brien, "From French to English," in Brower, *On Translation*, 90.

9. Jean Paris, "Translation and Creation," in Arrowsmith and Shattuck, *Craft and Context*, 57; Clive Scott, "Translating the Literary: Genetic Criticism, Text Theory and Poetry," in Bassnett and Bush, *Translator as Writer*, 113–114.

10. Ibid., 114.

11. Paul Blackburn, interviewed in *The Poet's Craft: Interviews from the New York Quarterly*, ed. W. Packard, quoted by Venuti, *Translator's Invisibility*, 246.

Chapter 7

1. Anna Akhmatova, quoted in Hanne, "Metaphors," 217.

2. The actual quote is: "I like to say, guardedly, that I could define poetry this way: it is that which is lost out of both prose and verse in translation." Robert Frost, *Conversations on the Craft of Poetry* (New York: Holt, Rinehart, and Winston, 1961), 7.

3. Paul Valéry, "A Solemn Address," quoted by Jackson Mathews, "Third Thoughts on Translating Poetry," in Brower, *On Translation*, 74; Rexroth, "Poet as Translator," 171.

4. Thirlwell, *Delighted States*, 5.

5. Edouard Roditi, "The Poetics of Translation," *Poetry* 60 (1942), 33; W. S. Merwin, interview by Christopher Merrill (2001), in *TTP*, 466–467; Yves Bonnefoy, "On the Translation of Form in Poetry," ibid., 468.

6. Merwin, interview with Merrill, 466–467; Clarence Brown, introduction to *Selected Poems of Osip Mandelstam*, in *TTP.*, 464–465.

7. Douglas Robinson, "The Ascetic Foundations of Western Translatology," in *TTP*, 537–538.

8. Ezra Pound, "Notes on Elizabethan Classicists," in *TTP*, 275. See also 274.

9. Rexroth, "Poet as Translator," 187.

10. Eliot Weinberger and Octavio Paz, *19 Ways of Looking at Wang Wei* (Kingston, RI: Asphodel, 1987), 9. See the entire volume for a fascinating glimpse of the many translations one can derive from a single Chinese poem. In a review of David Hinton's *Classical Chinese Poetry: An Anthology*, Adam Kirsch shows that some of Hinton's more scholarly renderings are "not very different from Pound's" ("Disturbances of Peace," *New Republic*, May 20, 2009, accessed May 27, 2017, https:// newrepublic.com/article/60991/disturbances-peace). For the different versions of Li Po's poem in the following paragraphs, see "Other Translations of 'A River Merchant's Wife,' " *Modern American Poetry*, accessed

April 2, 2017, http://www.english.illinois.edu/maps/poets/m_r/pound/othertranslations.htm.

11. Steiner, *After Babel*, 359.

12. Ezra Pound, letter to W. H. D. Rouse (1935), in *TTP*, 281.

13. Robert Lowell, introduction to *Imitations* (New York: Farrar, Straus, and Giroux, 1961), xi–xii; Abraham Cowley, "Preface to 'Pindarique Odes' " (1656), quoted by Nida, *Toward a Science*, 17.

14. Robert Lowell, interview with D. S. Carne Ross, quoted in *TTP*, 352; "things profoundly offensive": Guy Daniels, "The Tyranny of Free Translation," *Translation* 1, no. 1 (winter 1973), 17–18.

15. "We must dismiss": Vladimir Nabokov, foreword to *A Hero of Our Time*, in *TTP*, 382; "a crime": Nabokov, "Art of Translation," 3.

16. "Clumsiest literal translation" and "I want translations": Vladimir Nabokov, "Problems of Translation: *Onegin* in English," in Schulte and Biguenet, *Theories of Translation*, 127, 143; "greatest poem": Nabokov, quoted in *TTP*, 388; "to my ideal" and "render the 'spirit' ": Nabokov, translator's foreword to Aleksandr Pushkin, *Eugene Onegin: A Novel in Verse*, vol. 1 (Princeton, NJ: Princeton University Press, 1975), ix–x.

17. Vladimir Nabokov, "On a Book Entitled *Lolita*," in *TTP*, 378.

18. "The Cloak of Genius," *Time*, February 21, 1969.

19. Alexander Gerschenkron, "A Magnificent Monument?," quoted in Steiner, *After Babel*, 315n; Dudley Fitts, "The Poetic Nuance," in Brower, *On Translation*, 34; Nabokov, "Art of Translation," 8–9.

20. "The best translations": Edmund Wilson, *The Nabokov-Wilson Letters*, quoted in *TTP*, 382; "a disappointment": Edmund Wilson, "The Strange Case of Pushkin and Nabokov," *New York Review of Books*, July 15, 1965, accessed October 22, 2017, https://www.nybooks.com/articles/1965/07/15/the-strange-case-of-pushkin-and-nabokov/; Vladimir Nabokov, "Reply to My Critics," in *TTP*, 390. See also Jeffrey Meyers, *Edmund Wilson: A Biography* (Boston: Houghton Mifflin, 1995), 435–450.

21. Isaiah Berlin, letter to Edmund Wilson, January 25, 1966, quoted by Meyers, *Edmund Wilson*, 444–445.

Chapter 8

1. Bellos, 145.

2. André Breton, "Manifesto of Surrealism," in *Manifestoes*, 32; Breton, "Words without Wrinkles," in *The Lost Steps*, trans. Mark Polizzotti (Lincoln: University of Nebraska Press, 1996), 102.

3. Breton, "Manifesto of Surrealism," 39.

4. Jean-Pierre Brisset, "The Great Law, or The Key to Speech," in André Breton, *Anthology of Black Humor*, trans. Mark Polizzotti (San Francisco: City Lights Books, 1987), 186. See also 181–188.

5. See Claire Davison-Pégon, "L'intraduisible comme revanche du nonsens? Le cas d'Artaud, traducteur," *Les chantiers de la création* 1 (2008), accessed April 9, 2017, http://lcc.revues.org/125.

6. This and the following two paragraphs: Louis Wolfson, *Le schizo et les langues* (Paris: Gallimard, 1970), 61–63, 213, 70. Translations are my own.

7. J. M. G. Le Clézio, "La tour de Babil," in *Dossier Wolfson, ou L'affaire du "Schizo et les langues"* (Paris: Gallimard, 2009), 46, 48. See also 21.

Chapter 9

1. Nina Martyris, " 'Paradise Lost': How the Apple Became the Forbidden Fruit," *The Salt* (blog), *National Public Radio*, April 30, 2017, accessed June 23, 2017, http://www.npr.org/sections/thesalt/2017/04/30/526069512/paradise-lost-how-the-apple-became-the-forbidden-fruit/.

2. Kelly and Zetzsche, *Found in Translation*, 113; Weinberger, "Anonymous Sources," 28–29. Sometimes even correct translations cling to posterity as indelible mistakes, among them John F. Kennedy's famous "jelly doughnut" declaration—whereas in fact, *Ich bin ein Berliner* says

exactly what Kennedy meant: that he was a fellow citizen of Berlin. But the doughnut makes for a better story, if not better history. See *Found in Translation*, 57–58.

3. Kelly and Zetzsche, *Found in Translation*, 44.

4. Grossman, x.

5. Weinberger, "Anonymous Sources," 18; George Steiner, introduction to *The Penguin Book of Modern Verse Translation* (New York: Penguin, 1966), 25.

6. Thirlwell, *Delighted States*, 373–374.

Selected Bibliography

Allen, Esther, and Susan Bernofsky, eds. *In Translation: Translators on Their Work and What It Means*. New York: Columbia University Press, 2013.

Apter, Emily. *The Translation Zone: A New Comparative Literature*. Princeton, NJ: Princeton University Press, 2006.

Arrowsmith, William, and Roger Shattuck, eds. *The Craft and Context of Translation*. Austin: University of Texas Press, 1961.

Artaud, Antonin. "NEANT OMO NOTAR NEMO" [based on "Jabberwocky"]. In *Œuvres complètes, IX*. Paris: Gallimard, 1971.

Bassnett, Susan. *Translation Studies*. Rev. ed. London: Routledge, 1991.

Bassnett, Susan. *Translation*. London: Routledge, 2014.

Bassnett, Susan, and Peter Bush, eds. *The Translator as Writer*. New York: Continuum, 2006.

Beckett, Samuel, trans. "Simulation of General Paralysis Essayed" by André Breton and Paul Éluard. In *This Quarter: Surrealist Number* (1932). Reprint: New York: Arno Press, 1969.

Bellos, David. *Is That a Fish in Your Ear? Translation and the Meaning of Everything*. New York: Faber and Faber, 2011.

Benjamin, Walter. *Illuminations*. Translated by Harry Zohn. New York: Schocken, 1969.

Bermann, Sandra, and Michael Wood, eds. *Nation, Language, and the Ethics of Translation*. Princeton, NJ: Princeton University Press, 2005.

Biguenet, John, and Rainer Schulte, eds. *The Craft of Translation*. Chicago: University of Chicago Press, 1989.

Brower, Reuben A., ed. *On Translation*. Cambridge, MA: Harvard University Press, 1959.

Carroll, Lewis. *Tout Alice*. Translated by Henri Parisot. Paris: Flammarion, 1979.

Echenoz, Jean. *Big Blondes*. Translated by Mark Polizzotti. New York: New Press, 1997. Revised version in *Three by Echenoz*. New York: New Press, 2014.

Eco, Umberto. *Experiences in Translation*. Translated by Alastair McEwen. Toronto: University of Toronto Press, 2001.

Findlay, Jean. *Chasing Lost Time: The Life of C. K. Scott Moncrieff, Soldier, Spy, and Translator*. New York: Farrar, Straus, and Giroux, 2015.

Flaubert, Gustave. *Bouvard and Pécuchet* [no translator given]. London: M. Walter Dunne, 1904.

Flaubert, Gustave. *Bouvard and Pécuchet*. Translated by T. W. Earp and G. W. Stonier. New York: New Directions, 1954.

Flaubert, Gustave. *Bouvard and Pécuchet*. Translated by A. J. Krailsheimer. New York: Penguin, 1976.

Flaubert, Gustave. *Bouvard and Pécuchet*. Translated by Mark Polizzotti. Champaign, IL: Dalkey Archive Press, 2005.

Grossman, Edith. *Why Translation Matters*. New Haven, CT: Yale University Press, 2010.

Howard, Richard, trans. "Madness: An Attempt to Simulate General Paralysis" by André Breton and Paul Éluard. In Maurice Nadeau, *The History of Surrealism*. New York: Macmillan, 1965.

Kelly, Nataly, and Jost Zetzsche. *Found in Translation: How Language Shapes Our Lives and Transforms the World*. New York: Perigee, 2012.

Kundera, Milan. *Testaments Betrayed: An Essay in Nine Parts*. New York: HarperPerennial, 1996.

Lê, Linda. *The Three Fates*. Translated by Mark Polizzotti. New York: New Directions, 2010.

Levine, Suzanne Jill. *The Subversive Scribe: Translating Latin American Fiction*. Saint Paul, MN: Graywolf, 1991.

Lowell, Robert. *Imitations*. New York: Farrar, Straus, and Giroux, 1961.

Nabokov, Vladimir. *Verses and Versions: Three Centuries of Russian Poetry*. Edited by Brian Boyd and Stanislav Shvabrin. New York: Harcourt, 2008.

Nida, Eugene A. *Toward a Science of Translating*. Leiden, the Netherlands: E. J. Brill, 1964.

Nirenburg, Sergei, Jaime Carbonell, Masaru Tomita, and Kenneth Goodman. *Machine Translation: A Knowledge-Based Approach*. San Mateo, CA: Morgan Kaufmann, 1992.

Parks, Tim. *Translating Style*. 2nd ed. London: Routledge, 2014.

Perec, Georges. *A Void*. Translated by Gilbert Adair. Boston: David R. Godine, 2005.

Pound, Ezra. *Poems and Translations*. Edited by Richard Sieburth. New York: Library of America, 2003.

Pushkin, Alexander. *The Poems, Prose and Plays of Alexander Pushkin*. Edited by Avrahm Yarmolinsky. New York: Modern Library, 1936.

Pushkin, Aleksandr. *Eugene Onegin: A Novel in Verse*. Translated by Vladimir Nabokov. Princeton, NJ: Princeton University Press, 1975.

Rabassa, Gregory. *If This Be Treason: Translation and Its Dyscontents*. New York: New Directions, 2006.

Rexroth, Kenneth. *World Outside the Window: The Selected Essays of Kenneth Rexroth*. Edited by Bradford Morrow. New York: New Directions, 1987.

Ricoeur, Paul. *On Translation*. Translated by Eileen Brennan. London: Routledge, 2006.

Rimbaud, Arthur. *Complete Works, Selected Letters*. Translated by Wallace Fowlie. Chicago: University of Chicago Press, 1966.

Roche, Maurice. *Compact*. Translated by Mark Polizzotti. Elmwood Park, IL: Dalkey Archive Press, 1988.

Roussel, Raymond. *How I Wrote Certain of My Books*. Translated by Trevor Winkfield. New York: SUN, 1977.

Roussel, Raymond. *Impressions of Africa*. Translated by Mark Polizzotti. Champaign, IL: Dalkey Archive Press, 2011.

Savory, Theodore H. *The Art of Translation*. London: Jonathan Cape, 1957.

Schulte, Rainer, and John Biguenet, eds. *Theories of Translation: An Anthology of Essays from Dryden to Derrida*. Chicago: University of Chicago Press, 1992.

Steiner, George. *After Babel: Aspects of Language and Translation*. New York: Oxford University Press, 1975.

Thirlwell, Adam. *The Delighted States*. New York: Picador, 2010.

Turle, Bernard. *Diplomat, Actor, Translator, Spy*. Cahier 19. Paris: Center for Writers and Translators, American University of Paris, 2013.

van Rooten, Luis d'Antin, ed. *Mots d'heures: Gousses, rames*. New York: Penguin, 1980.

Venuti, Lawrence. *The Translator's Invisibility: A History of Translation*. London: Routledge, 1995.

Venuti, Lawrence. *The Scandals of Translation: Towards an Ethics of Difference*. London: Routledge, 1998.

Venuti, Lawrence, ed. *The Translation Studies Reader*. 2nd ed. London: Routledge, 2004.

Weinberger, Eliot, and Octavio Paz. *19 Ways of Looking at Wang Wei*. Kingston, RI: Asphodel, 1987.

Weissbort, Daniel, and Astradur Eysteinsson, eds. *Translation—Theory and Practice: A Historical Reader*. New York: Oxford University Press, 2006.

Wolfson, Louis. *Le schizo et les langues*. Paris: Gallimard, 1970.

Index

For the reader's convenience, topics specifically related to the process of translation have been gathered under the entry "Translation."